PHILIP
WILSON STEER

Philip Wilson Steer by Walter Sickert, c.1895

PHILIP WILSON STEER

Ysanne Holt

Border Lines Series Editor
John Powell Ward

SEREN BOOKS

SEREN BOOKS is the book imprint of
Poetry Wales Press Ltd
Andmar House, Tondu Road, Bridgend, Mid Glamorgan

British Library Cataloguing in Publication Data

Holt, Ysanne
  Philip Wilson Steer. - (Border Lines Series)
  I. Title II. Series
  759.2
          ISBN 1-85411-073-X
          ISBN 1-85411-074-8 paperback

*The publisher acknowledges the financial assistance of the Welsh Arts
Council*

Cover illustration: 'Chepstow Castle', 1905, by Philip Wilson Steer

Typeset in Plantin by Megaron, Cardiff

Printed and bound by WBC, Bridgend, Mid Glam.

Other Titles in the Border Lines Series

Bruce Chatwin
Eric Gill and David Jones at Capel-y-Ffin
A. E. Housman
Francis Kilvert
Mary Webb
Samuel Sebastian Wesley
Raymond Williams

CONTENTS

List of Illustrations

Series Preface

The Border country is that region between England and Wales which is upland and lowland, both and neither. Centuries ago kings and barons fought over these Marches without their national allegiance ever being settled. In our own time, referring to his own childhood, that eminent borderman Raymond Williams once said: 'We talked of "The English" who were not us, and "The Welsh" who were not us.' It is beautiful, gentle, intriguing, and often surprising. It displays majestic landscapes, which show a lot, and hide some more. People now walk it, poke into its cathedrals and bookshops, fly over or hang-glide from its mountains, yet its mystery remains.

In cultural terms the region is as fertile as (in parts) its agriculture and soil. The continued success of the Three Choirs Festival and the growth of the border town of Hay as a centre of the secondhand book trade have both attracted international recognition. The present series of introductory books is offered in the light of such events. Writers as diverse as Mary Webb, Raymond Williams and Wilfred Owen are seen in the special light — perhaps that cloudy, golden twilight so characteristic of the region — of their origin in this area or association with it. There are titles too, though fewer, on musicians and painters. The Gloucestershire composers such as Samuel Sebastian Wesley, and painters like David Jones, bear an imprint of border woods, rivers, villages and hills.

How wide is the border? Two, five or fifteen miles each side of the boundary; it depends on your perspective, on the placing of the nearest towns, on the terrain itself, and on history. In the time of Offa and after, Hereford itself was a frontier town, and Welsh was spoken there even in the nineteenth century. True border folk traditionally did not recognize those from even a few miles away.

Today, with greater mobility, the crossing of boundaries is easier, whether for education, marriage, art or leisure. For myself, who spent some childhood years in Herefordshire and much of the past ten crossing between England and Wales once a week, I can only say that as you approach the border you feel it. Suddenly you are in that finally elusive terrain, looking from a bare height down on to a plain, or from the lower land up to a gap in the hills, and you want to explore it, maybe not to return.

This elusiveness pertains to the writers and artists too. Did the urbane Elizabeth Barrett Browning, just outside Ledbury till her late twenties, have a border upbringing? Are the 'English pastoral' composers, with names like Parry, Howells, and Vaughan Williams, English, or are they indeed Welsh? One wonders whether border country is now suddenly found on the English side of the Severn Bridge, and how far even John Milton's *Comus*, famous for its first production in Ludlow Castle, is in any sense such a work. Then there is the fascinating Uxbridge-born Peggy Eileen Whistler, transposed in the 1930s into Margiad Evans to write her visionary novels set near her adored Ross-on-Wye and which today still retain a magical charm. Further north: could Barbara Pym, born and raised in Oswestry, even remotely be called a border writer? Most people would say that the poet A.E. Housman was far more so, yet he hardly ever visited the county after which his chief book of poems, *A Shropshire Lad*, is named. Further north still: there is the village of Chirk on the boundary itself, where R.S. Thomas had his first curacy; there is Gladstone's Hawarden library, just outside Chester and actually into Clwyd in Wales itself; there is intriguingly the Wirral town of Birkenhead, where Wilfred Owen spent his adolescence and where his fellow war poet the Welsh Eisteddfod winner Hedd Wyn was awarded his Chair — posthumously.

On the Welsh side the names are different. The mystic Ann Griffiths; the metaphysical poet Henry Vaughan; the astonishing nineteenth century symbolist novelist Arthur Machen (in Linda Dowling's phrase, 'Pater's prose as registered by Wilde'); and the remarkable Thomas Olivers of Gregynog, author of the well-known hymn 'Lo he comes with clouds descending'. Those descending clouds . . . ; in border country the scene hangs overhead, and it is easy to indulge in inaccuracies. Most significant perhaps is the difference to the two peoples on either side. From

England, the border meant the enticement of emptiness, a strange unpopulated land, going up and up into the hills. From Wales, the border meant the road to London, to the university, or to employment, whether by droving sheep, or later to the industries of Birmingham and Liverpool. It also meant the enemy, since borders and boundaries are necessarily political. Much is shared, yet different languages are spoken, in more than one sense.

With certain notable exceptions, the books in this series are short introductory studies of one person's work or some aspect of it. There are no footnotes or indexes. The bibliography lists main sources referred to in the text, and sometimes others, for anyone who would like to pursue the topic further. The authors reflect the diversity of their subjects. They are specialists or academics; critics or biographers; poets or musicians themselves; or ordinary people with however an established reputation of writing imaginatively and directly about what moves them. They are of various ages, both sexes, Welsh and English, border people themselves or from further afield.

Philip Wilson Steer was awarded the Order of Merit in 1931. He was the acknowledged leader of Impressionism in Britain, and already in his own lifetime held to be the natural heir of Constable and Turner. Steer's paintings of the East Anglian landscape where Constable had flourished, and his paintings of border country spots — Chepstow and Ludlow, the Severn and the Wye — rendered by Turner, illustrate this inheritance conveniently enough. The Turneresque qualities of light in Steer's Ludlow and Severn studies have particular relevance for earlier remarks in this preface.

Ysanne Holt's study of Steer, however, places him in his proper rank as a painter of national and international stature. This is the first study in any length of Steer since Bruce Laughton's Oxford edition in 1971, and only the third ever. The first was by Steer's friend D.S. McColl, Keeper of the Tate Gallery and on whom Ysanne Holt is an authority. It appeared in 1945, three years after Steer's death in 1942. That latter date also means that this present book's publication marks the fiftieth anniversary of Steer's death. This anniversary, the wider turn back toward representation in current painting, and the quality of Ysanne Holt's work, make this a timely publication in the border series.

John Powell Ward

Acknowledgements

The publishers thank the following galleries for their generosity and kind permission to reproduce the following illustrations. The Tate Gallery for 'Chepstow Castle' (front cover), 'What of the War?', 'The Swiss Alps at the Earls Court Exhibition', 'The Bridge', 'Girls Running, Walberswick Pier', 'Richmond Castle', 'Nutting', 'The Outskirts of Montreuil', 'The River, Ironbridge', 'Mrs Raynes' and 'Low Tide, Greenhithe'; The National Portrait Gallery for 'Phillip Wilson Steer' by Walter Sickert; Ipswich Borough Council Museums and Galleries for 'Knucklebones, Walberswick'; Chris Beetles Ltd, St James's, London for 'Classic Landscape'; the City Art Gallery, Manchester, for 'The Embarkment'; the Imperial War Museum for 'Dover Harbour, 1918', Williamson Art Gallery and Museum for 'Girl's Head in Profile'.

I
1860 – 1892

Youth and the Appeal of France

Writing in 1924 the modernist critic Roger Fry claimed Philip Wilson Steer was "one of the most gifted and purest artists that we have ever had in England". This comment, coming from one associated with the most advanced developments in French art, may initially seem bizarre. But Steer's painting consistently evoked extreme reactions, positive or otherwise.

The painter himself, an excessively mild and modest individual, appears to be a strange candidate for such remarks. He always played down his own artistic talent, with a parallel talent for self mockery: "Forty years of a wasted life", he said, "forty years I have painted thick and I should have painted thin".

Philip Wilson Steer's years as a painter span a particularly interesting period in the recent history of British art. During his lifetime painters in this country took on some of the challenges in art that had effectively been established by those working in France. In accepting these challenges they were initially forced to contend with an extremely nationalistic, almost xenophobic climate of opinion at home, that sought constantly to maintain the isolationism which had characterised British painting for much of the nineteenth century.

Yet this is not a straightforward history of a progression from complete rejection to final acceptance of the ideals of a seemingly radical group of artists. What fascinates about this period is the gradual and complex process by which national and cultural values reassert themselves at specific moments and within particular groups of individuals. Within this process ideals are co-opted and intentions are subtly transformed until the established climate — the main body of opinion — and the once seemingly rebellious spirits converge, contentions subside to be taken up in different forms by new forces.

13

Steer's career is a fascinating example of this process. Almost in spite of himself, in his art and in the circles within which he moved, he is a touchstone for the experience and preoccupations of his generation. With a deliberate tenacity and a total lack of theoretical pomposity, Steer in his early days took on board artistic concerns that were quite outside the conventional perceptions of painting at home. For this he received possibly more hostile criticism than any of his contemporaries. Yet in the shifts and turns of his work in later years, and in its ultimate success with a much wider public, Steer reflected and refined many of the features of cultural life of the time. A sense of nostalgia for the ideals of the past, a romantic attachment to an image of rural life and rural scenery, in his case to the landscape of his childhood in the Welsh Borders, and an interest in a tradition which could also finally be interpreted as nationalistic. All of these aspects of his paintings were to feature in the art and also the literature of a good many others, and found an increasingly sympathetic response. A chord was struck and assimilation developed.

This study of Steer aims to discuss the development of the artist in relation to the wider themes and preoccupations of the era and to the changing critical perception of British art.

Steer was born in Birkenhead in 1860, the youngest of three children; the eldest a sister, Catherine, and a brother, Henry. Their mother, Emma, was the daughter of an heiress and sometime watercolourist, Mary Hornsby, and a clergyman, William Harrison, who settled as a curate in Shropshire. Emma Harrison met her husband, Philip Steer, through attending his painting classes in Bideford.

Philip Steer was noted mainly as a portrait painter, and was descended from a farming background, although his family had also established a firm of shipbuilders in New York. His training in art came initially from a neighbour at his home in Devonshire, but he was soon taken up by a local baronet and art enthusiast, Sir William Elford, who encouraged his interest in portraiture, and urged him to study Reynolds in particular. His own work reflected a preoccupation with the styles of the eighteenth century both in his portraits and landscapes — a period in art which would absorb his youngest son also in later years. After marriage in 1853 the couple moved to Birkenhead where Philip Steer continued to teach. Emma

Steer fell ill shortly after her last son's birth, and the child was largely cared for by the family's Welsh nurse Jane Raynes. After the death of her husband Jane returned to the family service and remained with Steer until her own death in 1929. She was a powerful, indomitable presence.

As a baby Steer had suffered badly from bronchitis. This illness recurred periodically and led to a hypochondriacal concern for his own health that lasted throughout his life and which he often took to quite ludicrous lengths, to the amusement of acquaintances.

When Steer was four years old the family moved to Ross-on-Wye, to Apsley House in Whitchurch. There the children led a seemingly idyllic existence and Steer recalled the long rambles with his father around Herefordshire and the collection of shells, plants and minerals made on these walks which they arranged in a museum at home. This typically nineteenth century love for the natural sciences remained throughout Steer's life as did an affection for that particular landscape — its rolling hills and open skies.

Philip Steer died in 1871 when Steer was eleven, and four years later he followed his brother Henry to Hereford Cathedral School where he remained for two years. After a brief dalliance with the idea of joining the British Museum's Coin Department — an interest he had developed from his sister's husband, Charles Hamilton — in 1878 he began to study for civil service exams, work which he found dull and difficult, and readily abandoned. He was in fact consistently bored by academic work throughout his life. By this point, however, painting had emerged as a definite interest, one that had been encouraged by his father from Steer's earliest years. A picture of a dead bullfinch produced when he was fifteen showed marked promise, and in a self portrait of 1878, painted in the style of Reynolds, and sporting cloak and wide-brimmed hat, he had presented himself already in the guise of romantic young artist. Later that year he enrolled at Gloucester College of Art. Her two eldest children having left home, Emma Steer soon moved to Gloucester to be with her son, and the two set up house a short distance from the college.

Steer had considerable respect for the Principal at Gloucester at that time, John Kemp, and painted the portrait of him which is still owned by the college. Kemp maintained an interest in Steer's development for years to follow, writing a congratulatory letter at the time of his first one-man exhibition in 1894. Kemp's brother-in-law had also modelled for the old man reading a newspaper in *What of the War*, painted in 1882 and exhibited at the Royal Academy the next year, where the picture apparently remained unsold for some time at twenty guineas until a friend suggested raising the price to thirty, whereupon it sold almost immediately. For a short while in 1880 Steer attended the South Kensington drawing schools and gained a second grade certificate in perspective. From there, as was common practice, he applied to join the Royal Academy schools in 1882, but was unsuccessful. This rejection perhaps fuelled his later antipathy to the Academy and his lack of interest in their advances to him in subsequent years.

By deciding at the age of twenty-two to travel to Paris and enrol at the Academie Julian, Steer was acting in accordance with many young would-be artists of the 1880s. Some, like him, were rejected by the Royal Academy, and others making a conscious choice in favour of French methods of training — as opposed to the dull and increasingly archaic methods practised in the English schools. The decision these students made reflected both professional interests and wider social concerns.

Training at the Academy schools was characterised by a preoccupation with figure drawing and many long hours were spent in front of plaster casts and statues. The major figures at the Royal Academy were classicists, and as such study of the antique was of great importance in the search for the ideal perception of the nude. Ingrained in this tradition was also the concern for achieving a high finish in paintings. Students would spend many tedious hours stippling their canvases with pointed chalk pencils in an effort to create the slick surface smoothness that constituted the standard of excellence at the Royal Academy. One young artist, typical of the period, later recalled that:

> a drawing two feet to a yard high could take anything from three months to a year to complete, and the one which took a year was likely to be considered a masterpiece (ASH 1937 145).

And yet in spite of the time taken, the essentials of good drawing were lacking. This devotion to surface disguised the fact that little attempt was made to train a student's eye to observe the essential movement of the figure or to capture the character of the line — all qualities considered prerequisite to drawing in subsequent years, and at the Slade school in particular, where under the guidance of Alphonse Legros, a great draughtsman himself, students were taught to draw freely, "building up [. . .] drawings by observing the broad planes of the model" (WR 1929 77). Under Legros' professorship aspects of French training were established at the Slade and these allowed a greater degree of freedom, with more drawing from live models and less endless copying in the antique rooms.

But just as the training in British schools proved frustrating to Steer's contemporaries, so also did the content of much later Victorian painting. The subject matter of the most popular pictures, by artists such as Lord Leighton, Alma Tadema, Poynter and David Wilkie, sprang very much from the nineteenth century obsession with an historical and mythological past, with a frequent tendency to moralising anecdote and a fondness for sentimentality, often cloyingly overdone.

The artists amongst whom Steer must be counted formed part of a transitional movement, a shift away from the perceived aspects of 'Victorianism'. They developed an outlook that was for the most part at odds with that of their parents' generation, and as such adopted some of the *fin de siecle* spirit of the following decade — years in which Holbrook Jackson was to observe a passing:

> not only from one social system to another, but from one morality to another, from one culture to another, and from one religion to a dozen or none (HJ 1939 27–28).

The attractions of Paris therefore lay also in this reaction of youth against the cultural condition of home, from the rigid codes of social behaviour, and the repressive conservatism of late nineteenth century England. Paris was an international art centre and a Mecca for artists from England and also from America. This disappearance of the nation's talent across the channel was much noted at the time, not unsympathetically by some, but by all with a sense of alarm. One writer, the Academy painter P.H. Calderon, warned against this 'perfect mania' and appealed to a spirit of patriotic pride in his country's youth. He expressed concern that by staying abroad at such vulnerable ages:

your English feelings and reticences imperceptibly fall away . . . .
you find you have lost touch, as it were, with the intellect of your
native country, and . . . . you are as a stranger in your own land
(PHC 1884 58–9).

Unfortunately for Calderon that was just part of the attraction
for many. Steer's friend Walter Sickert later commented that Paris
was where "ideas count, where the town is stirred by a man, by an
article, by a question of style, of wit" (CC 1965 167). A deliberate
exaggeration no doubt, but nonetheless an indication at least of the
superficial appeal of the city from across the Channel. It would
appear, however, that the image Sickert presented was not quite the
experience of a good many of the ex-patriots, and ultimately
certainly not of Steer.

The Academie Julian was the most popular of the art schools
attended by the English and Americans. At the time it was the
largest art school in Paris, with some 4,000 enrolled by the mid
eighties. It was opened originally in 1868 by one described as a
painter-manqué and ex-strong man, who simply hired a studio,
engaged a model, and managed to persuade several well known
patrons to correct the students' efforts — for a fee.

George Moore, a member of Steer's circle of friends in later
years, remembered the atmosphere in the studio — some eighteen
or twenty men, sitting in a circle and drawing from the model. This
reversal, he wrote, "of all the world's opinions and prejudices was
to me singularly delightful" (GM 1917 14).

In spite of this apparent air of bohemian informality the vast
majority of the students led fairly insular lives, often remaining in
their own cliques, and usually with little involvement, even little
awareness, of many current developments in French art. This was
particularly the case for Steer. He remained very much within
limited circles, his main companions at Julian's were T.B.
Kennington and James Christie. Although he enjoyed Paris he
ventured little further than the studio and his hotel room, money
being one factor and difficulties with language another. In letters to
his mother and his brother Henry he talked of the fleas and the
stench of the streets and often of the weather. But in terms of his
studies he seemed more positive, gradually finding his feet in the
studio, improving his drawing and spending afternoons in the
Louvre. He was undoubtedly a conscientious student, spending

Christmas Day at work on his study for the Concours, a monthly event with a first prize of one hundred francs.

Steer's tutor at Julian's was the popular classicist and academic salon painter William-Adolphe Bouguereau, who visited the studios only once or twice each week and appears not to have been exceptionally forthcoming in his criticisms. Certainly most stimulating discussion would have taken place among the student coteries themselves.

Steer's isolation from avant-garde French art was brought about partly by the language problem, and at this point no doubt also by a lack of appreciative ability. This meant that he would have known little or nothing of the development of Impressionism despite the fact that the first Impressionist exhibition had taken place in Paris in 1874, eight years before he arrived there.

The technique with which he was the most familiar, in fact the 'house style' clearly identifiable with Julian's, was rustic naturalism. This was the style most associated with the peasant paintings of Bastien-Lepage, who painted in the villages of northern France, and had achieved a solid following by the time of his premature death in 1886. His was considered to be the most advanced form of painting at the start of the 1880s, appearing quite radical in content and technique. It was primarily a realist style, dealing on the whole with low life themes, taken from the daily lives of the rural poor. Pictures were produced on the spot, *en plein air*, and were characterised by a consistent grey light and by the use of square brushmarks worked across forms and by attention to tone and values at the expense of colour.

Rustic naturalism was of enormous consequence to Steer and other young painters studying in Paris during these years — such as Fred Brown, Edward Stott, George Clausen and John Lavery. It appeared quite revolutionary against the standard Academy pictures in England, the historical scenes and the fancy dress paintings, and so it is understandable that the work of Monet and Degas should have remained relatively obscure to them.

Strangely it was not until he returned home on holiday in 1883 that Steer most probably had his first encounter with Impressionism, at one of Durund-Ruel's exhibitions at Dowdeswell's gallery. There he could have seen several of Monet's landscapes, although no signs of influence from these works would be evident for several years in Steer's own paintings. The most significant show in terms of his own immediate progress was a posthumous exhibition of Manet's pictures in Paris in June 1884 to which Steer's initial reaction was mixed — being more impressed by landscapes, and finding the nudes "blown out looking things" (JEB 1937 133).

Having spent three months at Julian's atelier, Steer managed to enrol at the Ecole des Beaux Arts under Cabanel via an introduction arranged by a family friend. Despite much initial excitement at this move, expressed in letters to his brother, his enthusiasm seems to have waned fairly quickly. The studio was greatly overcrowded and there was a constant emphasis on copying, which he had always found to be 'dry work'. There is little documented information on Steer's time in Paris other than these letters, many of which were later destroyed. Of finished work he produced a portrait of his friend, H.W. Macauley, which he exhibited at the Salon of 1884, painted apparently in the sober style of Fantin Latour. In the summer of that year the authorities imposed an examination in French to be taken by all students at the Beaux Arts in an effort to cull the number of foreigners present. Steer, not surprisingly, failed the test and returned to England.

His mother, who had by then moved to London, continued to provide some financial support and Steer was able to set up studio in Manresa Road, Chelsea. At this point, accompanied by Edward Stott, he travelled to Walberswick, a resort on the Suffolk coast. Walberswick had been popular with painters since the 1860s and Walter Osborne was the most notable of those working there at the time. Known affectionately as Wobbleswig it particularly attracted disciples of Bastien-Lepage. One friend of Steer's, Frank Emanuel, on a visit there one day was puzzled by the large throng of young artists gathering around his work and discovered later that he bore a strong resemblance to the great French painter and had been mistaken for him. Steer's visit in 1884 was the first of several excursions there, and it was to provide the background for some of his most radically innovative painting at the end of the decade. It also heralded the first of the regular summer painting trips which would feature more and more significantly in his development.

The popularity of specific sites for outdoor painting, and the formation of the various 'artists colonies' like the one at Walberswick and more famously at Cockburnspath in the Scottish

20

Borders, and Newlyn on the Cornish coast, were phenomena which developed mainly out of the experiences of British artists when in France in the early 1880s. Following in the footsteps of Bastien-Lepage, many of these had travelled to particular spots in Brittany to paint rural subjects in their native environment, and simply continued the practice at home. Newlyn was especially favoured for its close resemblance to the coastline in Brittany. It is of consequence as well that the beginning of the 1880s was the height of the great agricultural depression. Unemployment and poor standards of living in the countryside had led to a continued process of emigration to the constantly expanding industrial cities. The sense of cultural loss engendered by this rural depopulation not only sparked off the succession of preservation and heritage societies which featured in subsequent decades, but also witnessed a growing nostalgia for an idealised view of rural existence. From this developed an increasing market amongst the new middle classes for scenes of the countryside, and perhaps more specifically at this date, peasant workers. It was in this spirit that paintings by Bastien-Lepage, Jules Breton and others working in a similar social background in France received a generally favourable reception when first shown in London in the early 1880s.

However for the young British disciples of rustic naturalism it was a perceived lack of overt sentimentality that was important about Bastien-Lepage's example. As George Clausen remarked:

> His attitude towards nature is one of studied impartiality . . . . His people stand before you and you feel that they must be true to the very life. He loves to place them in an even, open light, and simply accepting the ordinary conditions of his sitters, produces a surprisingly original result (A. Theuriet 1892 114).

It was this air of honest detachment that the French painters' English and Scottish followers aimed to achieve. From his example come the realist depictions of villagers involved in their daily activities. Steer produced his own version of this approach in *Girl at a Well*, painted on that first visit to Walberswick. His picture is of a young girl in a red cap leaning against the village well. The subject and the positioning of the peasant girl squarely in the centre of the canvas with the background rising in steep planes, is strongly reminiscent of the style of Bastien-Lepage, and the same even light prevails.

Several of Steer's contemporaries, like Clausen himself, remained content to work in this idiom, with subtle variations, for many years to come. But for Steer, the search for fresh inspiration and influence, which characterises so much of his work, was clearly in evidence by the following year, 1885. His natural aversion to any kind of dogma in art meant that commitment to a particular style was bound to be short-lived. The most notable work of that year is his *Girl Leading Goats*. Problems arise with Steer's pictures often through inaccurate dating on the canvases. This one, marked 1887, has been re-dated and attributed to a trip across the Channel to France that summer. The site for the picture is identified as the low ridge of sand dunes at Etaples on the Normandy coast, not far from the more popular artists' centre around Dieppe. A place to which Steer would return later with his frequent painting companion, Fred Brown.

As a departure from the methods of the rustic naturalists, this large picture was worked up afterwards in the studio and altered at a later date. Although the subject is still typical of the naturalists, a more luminous quality in the paint indicates his developing interest in the effects of light, as against the consistent tonal quality of the naturalists.

The French landscape painter Cazin was acknowledged by Steer as an influence on the overall atmospheric quality of this picture of a girl leading her goats over a wide flat la.·dscape with the moon resting low on the horizon. Of particular note is this central image of an isolated female figure looking out into the distance, seen here for the first time. This image reappears in many of Steer's pictures through the 1890s, and despite fluctuating styles and techniques, it emerges as a dominant theme in his oeuvre. But at this point it was an image employed by several other painters — William Stott in particular in *The Ferry*, a painting of two young girls gazing across the river, praised for its poetic charm when shown at the Salon in 1882.

The appearance of the various artists' colonies that are so much a feature of this period, clearly developed out of an interest in the particular style and subject matter associated with the French painters that Steer's generation admired. Beyond this these communities also played an important role by providing a support network for young artists whose aims were largely dissimilar from those at the Academy, where classical nudes and set studio pieces continued to receive public acclaim and approval.

The formation of the New England Art Club (NEAC) in 1886, of which Steer was an initial and lifelong member, had a comparable role. And to a large extent the critical reaction to his work was tinged by public reaction to this institution itself, for at least the following decade. The great majority of the club's early members had, like Steer, trained in Paris at one time or another. Initially they all showed a typical reaction against the privileged status of the Royal Academy. W.J. Laidlay, whom Steer knew in Paris, and who was one of the club's prime movers, viewed the Academy as a

> narrow minded, self-seeking and self-interested clique, who safeguarded their position through their exclusion of innovative talent, to the detriment of a good national art (WJL 1907 52).

It functioned very much as a closed shop in the eyes of Steer and his circle, and as A.S. Hartrick later commented, was such a lucrative institution that "most members soon had their senses blunted by the richness of the sales" (ASH 1939 145). Hartrick records that a standard price to denote a masterpiece was somewhere in the region of 1,400 guineas, and any Academy artist who failed to sell at least one work each year for over £1,000 was thought to have failed. This perspective must be borne in mind in a consideration of painters like Steer himself, who for the first seven years of the NEAC sold virtually nothing, and continued to live off Emma Steer's allowance.

In accordance with their monetary successes Royal Academicians achieved high social status and their exalted position was often criticised, as here, by A.C.R. Carter:

> The innate love of institutions in this country has elevated the Royal Academy to such a pitch in the popular estimation that its members, who consider themselves as merely members of a smug and privileged club, are held outside to be a College of Art Cardinals (ACRC 1904 6).

Faced with such an entrenched system the NEAC's immediate role was to provide exhibition space for artists whose work would otherwise remain unseen. In his recollections of the early years of the Club, Fred Brown remarked that, as students in Paris, his friends would frequently join in criticism of the Royal Academy's management of exhibitions as compared to the French system. All Salon exhibitors elected their own selection committee, and the NEAC adopted this same method. Indeed the consistently French tone of the Club was reflected in the list of alternative names suggested at its inception, one significant example being 'The Society of Anglo-French Artists'.

It was Fred Brown who suggested Steer's inclusion in the Club's first list of members, having seen his *Girl Leading Goats* at the Society of British Artists show in the winter of 1885. Fred Brown was a consistent supporter of Steer throughout the various stages of his career, and the development of his own art bore signs of his friend's influence. Their backgrounds and early training also had much in common. Brown's father was also a painter and teacher, and like Steer, Brown also attended the South Kensington schools, and found this experience and the organisation of the institution stifling in the extreme: "every natural instinct of the student was perverted or frustrated" (FB 1930 154).

Having left the schools he began teaching and was appointed to the Westminster School of Art in 1877. In 1883 however he followed that steady flow of younger artists to Paris, to the atelier Julian, where he also became absorbed in the rustic naturalist style. By the later eighties he proved himself a lynchpin in organisations and was a prime mover in developments within the NEAC.

Early teething problems beset the initial organisation of the first NEAC show at the Dudley Galleries in 1886, and there was some uncertainty about possible public response. And yet although early reactions were not unfavourable, Steer fared particularly badly with his only exhibit, *Andante*, a rather restrained picture of three women musicians that could scarcely have caused offence. But *Andante* marked a move away from the rustic peasant pictures to a more modern naturalism, and Brown, who regarded Steer's picture as one of the best works in the exhibition, wrote that despite his own protests, *Andante* was placed high on a badly lit wall, for reasons he could not quite understand. As he went on:

There was nothing particularly novel about the picture, unless truth of tone united with good colour into a charming whole might be thought novel, as assuredly they were in the prevailing art of the day (ibid 270).

For Brown this action marked an immediate doubt on his own part as to the value of the Club and was an early sign of a developing partisanship "against a certain kind of work as compared with another kind, of which Steer's work was representative" (ibid). The treatment of his painting no doubt depressed Steer considerably, and he later destroyed the work. This was an early indication of the hostility his painting would arouse for several years to follow.

By far the largest contingent of these first exhibitors were working in the rustic naturalist style derived from Bastien-Lepage. Most notable in this context were members of the Newlyn School, which included Stanhope Forbes, T.B. Kennington, T.C. Gotch, and alongside these, George Clausen. Fred Brown's own exhibit was representative of this style: *Hard Times*, a very desolate image of an unemployed labourer sitting alone in a country inn. It was a style that had gradually increased in popularity since Bastien-Lepage's *Les Foins* was shown at the Grosvenor Gallery in 1880.

There is a sense in which this style of painting contained little outside the realms of acceptable Victorian taste. The rural subject matter was appealing but particularly, as was most often the case, landscape was merely a backdrop for depictions of the figure. And the figure was most often a pretty young woman or an attractive group of children. Many of the pictures in the first NEAC exhibitions were tinged with that sweetness and sentimentality which eventually overcame English adaptations of French naturalism. Paintings by Bastien-Lepage were characterised by an extreme attention to detail, which would gel in the English mind with Pre-Raphaelitism, and indeed the French painter had been a great admirer of the Pre-Raphaelites. And so while many French painters, Millet most obviously, were not easily appreciated by the British public, Bastien-Lepage and those who emulated his style could be sure of a more appreciative response.

George Clausen, who showed a picture of a shepherdess in the first exhibition, usefully summed up these contemporary attitudes to Bastien-Lepage while also accounting for his success:

> While landscape has entered as a matter of course into his rustic
> pictures, it was always subordinate to the figures, although he
> carried the finish of the foreground in these pictures to the
> furthest possible degree, delighting to express the beauty of
> everything — weeds, sticks, stones . . . . all was felt and shown to
> be beautiful (AT 1892 114).

Steer very quickly reacted against this meticulous attention to
detail as his subsequent pictures show. He also tired of the
conventional naturalist subject matter. The endless depiction of
cabbage plots and the like rapidly appeared clichéd and he was
particularly amused by the title of one typical painting by Francis
Bate — *Fine Rain Falls on Young Swedes*.

The extent to which his associates at the NEAC had absorbed the
lessons of Bastien-Lepage, his technical skill, his attention to detail
and also the strong sense of pathos in his pictures, was clear from
the positive tone of most reviews. Typical was the notice in *The
Times*, which noted the influence of French naturalism, but felt that
the British pictures showed a sincerity, a lack of theatrical display,
and a "preference for subjects that are beautiful rather than ugly,
which is English and not French" (WL 1907 203). This critical
perception of British art as drawn to beauty and French art to
ugliness, while laughable now, was very widespread. It was
common to view French representations as harsh and overly
realistic, and in this sense Bastien-Lepage was exempt from his
own tradition. The first NEAC show "succeeded in engrafting
English feeling and sentiment upon what is known as French
technique" (PMG 1886 71).

Yet it is still quite difficult to understand why Steer's rather
conventional handling of a polite middle class theme should have
been so badly treated. It seems this could only have been related to
his shift in subject matter, away from the by then commonplace
rustic images. Therefore Fred Brown's reaction and his suspicions
of a 'developing partisanship' seem justifiable.

Some dissatisfaction with the organisational powers within the
Club was made clear in the still early stages when a section of its
membership, headed by Henry Herbert La Thangue, proposed a
scheme for a public gallery with a committee elected from all artists
in the United Kingdom — a proposal which implicitly was a
criticism of the terms of the NEAC, which were too narrow in that

they were self-elected and had no natural mandate. The scheme came to nothing after some discussion, and, surprisingly perhaps after his own experience, Steer himself was "decidedly of the opinion that the Marlborough Gallery should continue on the same lines" (WL 1907 62). An early indication, this, of his natural reluctance to get embroiled in the art politics of his day; always content to leave debate and dissension to others while he stolidly got on with his painting. Jacques-Emile Blanche later remembered Steer from these early years, "smiling like a Buddha", he wrote, "he had the air of being upset if he had to give an opinion" (JEB 1937 133).

This is a period of rapid assimilation of styles and technique, whilst at the same time of the development of the theme which Steer continues through to the early 1890s — the girl looking into the distance, as seen in his *Girl Leading Goats* — but from this point set by the sea. This forms the basis of his 'On the Pierhead' series in which his method develops radically. The first of these is *Girl on a Pier*, painted in 1886. This is a *contre jour* painting in which the treatment of light emerges as one of Steer's main preoccupations. The brushwork is looser and has been related to Manet, although it is also typical of many paintings of the sea and could suggest pictures by several artists working on the French coast since Whistler, Courbet and Boudin in the 1860s.

At this stage Steer cannot be readily identified with one particularly dominating style, which in itself was possibly a reaction against the unified front of the rustic naturalists. As a consequence he maintained a detachment from cliques, and in 1887, despite a strong degree of stylistic influence, he was nevertheless keeping himself well apart from the circle of fervent admirers around Whistler; fearing apparently that excessive devotion could become a full-time occupation. Whistler himself, it seems, was "suspiciously aware of Steer from the first", and "liked courtiers better than possible rivals" (DSM 1945 36). So no direct contact was established between them. However, Whistler was an important figure for Steer, as he was for many in the next generation of painters at the NEAC.

Apart from his important formal and technical influence on subsequent painters, Whistler's personality, his sharp wit and merciless jibes at conventional taste and values, had a powerful impact on young artists in the mid-1880s. For impressionable critics like George Moore his writings were full of "glitter and go", of "sparkling and audacious epigrams" (GM 1893 2), and, his painting apart, for many his value lay equally in those verbal attacks on the grey conformity, respectability and monotony of much late Victorian social life. Whistler's example in this sense was crucial to the developing attacks on the 'Philistine', the moralising middle classes and the nouveaux riches, a theme which develops particularly in the nineties in the writings of Moore, MacColl and Sickert, all members of Steer's circle of friends and supporters.

The 'Philistine' ideology, which was the butt of Whistler's wit, was innate, in his eyes, in the attitudes to art and in the art institutions of the end of the nineteenth century. And any apparent upholders of this ideology, in particular staunchly conservative art critics like Harry Quilter, or ''Arry' as Whistler dubbed him, were obvious targets for his abuse.

Quilter was aggressive in his philistinism. On his own admission his art criticism was intended to address the widest possible public — to interest Tom, Dick, Harry et al. His perceptions on what constituted good art were fundamentally at odds with those of Whistler; and it was in the elaboration of these ideas, and the arguments that surrounded them, that Whistler's most serious significance lay. Clive Bell later described him as "a lonely artist" amongst the Londoners of the eighties:

> Overhaul the English art criticism of that time, from the cloudy rhetoric of Ruskin to the journalese of 'Arry and you will hardly find a sentence that gives ground for supposing that the writer has so much as guessed at what art is (KF 1984 238).

For Whistler it was not the business of art to be concerned with emotions such as pity or patriotism. It had no social function in the way that nineteenth century critics from Ruskin onwards had claimed. Art should appeal only to the aesthetic sensibility, and this was essentially the doctrine of 'art for art sake'. George Moore later echoed Whistler's view when he criticised the concern with historical detail and moral anecdote that continued to preoccupy Royal Academicians:

All the literature and all the sciences have been pressed into the
service of painting, and an Academy Catalogue is in itself a liberal
education . . . . the painter seems to have neglected nothing
except to learn how to paint (GM 1893 52).

For Steer, predominantly concerned with this last issue, the
formal qualities of Academy pictures, the obsession with finish and
accurate detail "rendered them like worms, which if you cut them
up they squirm and wriggle" (DSM 1945 177). According to
MacColl the 'playboy' part of Whistler, the spectacular dress,
quarrels, bailiffs, press campaigns and libel actions were distasteful
to Steer, who had first seen his paintings before leaving for Paris at
a Grosvenor Gallery exhibition in the late seventies. His first
reaction was to be "attracted but puzzled . . . . by his extreme
mistiness" (ibid 25).

Evidently by 1887 the mist must have cleared for Steer, and
several of his pictures of this date bear witness to the Whistlerian
approach. Steer's *Swiss Alps at the Earls Court Exhibition*, which he
exhibited at the NEAC in that year, is a case in point. The subject of
the picture is the painting of background scenery for the
switchback railway at the Earls Court Exhibition. Formally it bears
the hallmarks of Whistler's Nocturnes, painted in dark tones
thickly applied with sweeping brushstrokes and lightened with
touches of white. Steer was attracted to the harmonies and patterns
of design in Whistler's work. It is important to note that at this
point in the 1880s, and in many cases through the following decade,
the paintings of Whistler were generally perceived and judged to be
Impressionist paintings. But the artist himself never announced
any real affinity with Monet or Degas, and his work is clearly seen
now to be quite different in intentions and results. One of the
reasons for this critical confusion lay in the long term uncertainty as
to an exact definition of Impressionism. This uncertainty, and the
prejudice which it engendered, caused problems for the reception
of some of Steer's paintings in years to come, and may account for
the degree of hostility towards him in the press at the end of the
1880s.

In 1882 Whistler's painting was identified as Impressionist for
two reasons, viz:

it aims generally to record what the eye actually sees, and not what the mind knows the eye ought to see, and likewise, it addresses itself with courage and confidence to the artistic problems of our modern life, and our artificial society (KF 1984 45).

Steer's *Swiss Alps* can be seen to have addressed these same issues five years later also. In his full length portrait of Mrs Montgomery given the Whistlerian title *A Lady in Grey*, the model stands in that typically misty background that envelops Whistler's own portraits, and the overall concern with atmosphere, simplification and the selection of detail that characterises Whistler's painting is also apparent here.

Through Whistler's influence Steer learnt to eliminate some of the accumulation of visual fact that was a feature of earlier naturalist painting, and instead to aim towards a quality of harmony in the design. The technical means used to create such effects was Whistler's method of painting *alla prima* — layers of paint put down 'in one wet'. This technique inevitably led to a simplification in handling and detail and a lowering of tone. George Moore described how through Whistler's example art was "purged of the vice of subject and belief that the mission of the artist is to copy nature" (GM 1893 24). The lesson for artists was to distil visual poetry from nature rather than to slavishly reproduce its outward appearance.

Unlike friends such as Moore, Steer himself made few comments on the proper concerns of art. His attitudes are always best judged through his paintings themselves. His unwillingness to join in any critical debate, either in the press or at afternoon tea parties, earned him a reputation for intellectual idleness, or, more kindly, for reserve and integrity. As a result he tended to be viewed by outsiders via the pronouncements of his more vocal friends and acquaintances. This doubtless earned him criticism which was harder than he deserved from unsympathetic reviewers.

Despite his perceived stoicism Steer was obviously vulnerable to bad press. His longstanding friend, the painter Ronald Gray, remembered walking with him to Victoria Station some time in 1887: "He was depressed and said that he really felt like chucking painting because he never sold a picture and each time he exhibited he was abused" (DSM 1945 27). Yet there is no sign, at this stage, of Steer consciously modifying his art to make it more acceptable to a wider public. In fact the reverse is true, and in the last years of the 1880s and at the beginning of the next decade his work, if viewed in terms of a modernist progression, became increasingly radical in its style and technique.

A correlation between Steer's own mood at the time and the work he was producing may be found in the subject matter and the atmosphere of the most notable pictures of these years. The theme established earlier in 1886, of the young girl surveying a landscape, established itself as a dominant leitmotif in Steer's paintings. The best example, and probably the most successful, in my view, is *The Bridge*. This shows a back view of a young woman, leaning against the wooden bridge, looking across the water to a collection of fishing boats moored in a small harbour. In the extreme right of the picture a man in profile, apparently lost in his own thoughts, has not caught the woman's attention, which appears to be concentrated on the reflection of the boats' masts in the evening sunlight. The mirror-like effect of this light on the water is a prime concern in the work. The formal composition, the horizontal lines of the bridge and the horizon, the vertical lines of the figures, the masts and bridge supports, add to the stillness and calm of the overall atmosphere. And the woman herself, with that far-off gaze, lends an air of nostalgia, even of regret, to the picture — which is a characteristic of several of his pictures of this period.

Andrew Forge, in his catalogue on Steer, has identified qualities in *The Bridge* that anticipate the Nabi painting of a few years later (AF 1960 7). There is that sense of isolation, almost of loss in these paintings that is a feature also of the traditions of Northern Romantic painting, and the solitary watchers that appear in a stream of paintings dating from artists like Casper David Friedrich to Munch.

Possibly of more immediate relevance to Steer in this respect could be, again, the example of Whistler, who, in emulation of Courbet, had painted a back view of a figure peering out to sea at Trouville, albeit far more egotistically than in Steer's case. But the question raises itself as to whether Steer was simply aiming to create a similarly aesthetic evocation of emotion, or expressing some sense of alienated spiritual anguish in works like *The Bridge*. The recurrent nostalgia and the slight element of pathos in so many pictures of this period would suggest that the answer lies somewhere between the two, but his own mood faced with his hostile reception may be a contributory factor.

The response this picture received, when exhibited at the Grosvenor Gallery in 1888, can only have deepened Steer's depression. D.S. MacColl, who even in 1945 regarded the work merely as a "rather commonplace, but harmless enough scene . . .", recalled with amazement the *Daily Telegraph*'s description of it as "either a deliberate daub or so much more midsummer madness" (DSM 1945 26). And, as he went on to remark, Steer's period, after Whistler, as the most "contested painter of his time", had begun. In technical terms the influence on Steer is still Whistler, as the handling of the paint indicates, and the application is similar to that of the beach scenes at Etaples that Steer painted earlier in the summer.

In several other paintings of this year Steer dealt with the theme of childhood and innocence that typified the paintings of his Walberswick and Etaples period. Partly through the technical influence of Whistler, these pictures managed to avoid the overbearing sentimentality of so many Victorian renderings of similar themes. In one such, *Children Paddling, Etaples*, the children are painted almost as silhouettes in the sunlit sea, conveying also that quality of a romantic otherness — here combined with the unselfconsciousness that Steer associated with youth. A carefree vision but with an atmospheric resonance. George Moore identified the optimistic qualities of the painting when he described it, some years later in 1894, as a

> happy sensation of daylight; a flower-like afternoon; little children paddling; the world is behind them too; they are as flowers, and are conscious only of the benedictive influences of sand and sea (DSM 1945 185).

But Moore's obvious enthusiasm for this work was not shared by most contemporary critics, for whom paintings like these, which they defiantly associated with Impressionism, were garish, technically sloppy, badly composed and downright ugly.

In *Two Girls on the Pierhead*, most commonly identified as *On the Pierhead*, a similar mood to the previous two pictures is established. As in *The Bridge*, the two girls, their backs to the viewer, look out towards the boats at sea. The painting is interesting for its handling of the strong evening light where low sun casts long shadows behind the figures and the wooden post. These shadows add to the air of mystery and tension which imbues the work. While the painting technique may have more to do with Whistler, the strange perspective and the diagonal positioning of the girls is possibly due to the example of Degas, whose work would be mostly familiar to Steer through his developing friendship with Walter Sickert, whom he appears to have first met at the 1885–6 Society of British Artists exhibition referred to earlier. Through his relationship with Sickert in the late eighties Steer further identified himself in the public's mind with a radical faction in English painting.

Sickert and Steer were the same age exactly, and although their characters were very much at variance, there was an initial affinity between the two painters and a respect for each other's abilities which lasted throughout their lives, even when their attitudes towards subject differed sharply. Having abandoned an early career in acting Sickert enrolled at the Slade in 1881 but seems to have been largely unimpressed by tuition there. Very soon after his enrolment he was persuaded to leave by Whistler and became his assistant, helping him with his etchings, and carrying his stone on nightly trips to the Thames.

Whistler's forceful personality as well as his work clearly made a powerful early impression on Sickert, and the influence is present in the stylistic features of his own painting throughout the early 1880s, and in terms of an outspoken wit and dandyism for the rest of his life. In 1885 with an introduction from Whistler, Sickert met Degas in Paris and from this point the compositional effects and the subject matter of the French artist became apparent in Sickert's own pictures of the music halls of the later 1880s — a shift of allegiance that did not go down well with Whistler.

Sickert first became a member of the NEAC in 1888. For the growing contingent within that group who were dissatisfied with the developing conservatism of the original members, Sickert had a strong appeal — partly for his lively, rather anarchic character and partly for his personal contacts with two such significant artists.

The impact of Sickert is clear on Steer's *Signorine Sozo in 'Dresdina'* of 1887, a rare example of Steer's treatment of the music hall theme. The subject and the bizarre perspective of the picture, looking down from the balcony onto the dancer below, and the strong diagonal composition, are reminiscent of Degas via Sickert. The setting for the painting was the Alhambra music hall, and Steer and Sickert may have visited the performance of Signorine Sozo and Katie Lawrence (the latter a model for Sickert) together. At this stage the artists had substantial contact with each other and Steer later owned a series of Sickert's sketches from these years. Sickert quite often made Sunday visits to Emma Steer's house in Earls Court around 1889, and Steer visited Sickert and his first wife, Ellen Cobden, at their house in Midhurst. The two painted portraits of each other which they exhibited at the NEAC in 1891. Steer's portrait of Sickert, illustrated in the *Pall Mall Gazette* in 1890, is a rather formal half-length of his friend sporting a full moustache, while Sickert paints the young and still slim Steer relaxed in an armchair in front of a large propped up canvas.

Fred Brown, in his recollections, describes how by 1887–8, a group of dissatisfied members within the NEAC began to form a clique, which consisted of Brown himself, Steer, Starr, Roussel, Francis Bate and Sickert. The clique met at Sickert's house quite frequently and planned to become a dominating influence in the Club. By now the Club seemed to have lost much of its early radical promise, and many of its original members (for example several of the Newlyn Group, and Clausen) had begun to exhibit at the Royal Academy. This younger element continued their opposition to that institution. Sickert and Steer, for example, later took an advertisement in *The Times* to proudly announce they had once again been rejected by the Academy — a wheeze that was doubtless arranged by Sickert rather than Steer.

It was Sickert who invariably took the lead in the discussions that took place. Brown remembered the Sickert of those years: "his gaiety was contagious, his manners charming, his wit bubbly" (FB 1930 277). That carefree manner, while appealing to Steer, was often also an irritant at times, and he recounted in later years an incident which clearly annoyed him. On paying Steer a visit, Sickert chatted on for some time while the cab waited outside, its meter ticking away. Steer's 'economical instincts' were offended, especially as he had recently contributed to a subscription for Sickert who had at that point fallen upon hard times. One friend commented that Sickert invariably fell on his feet. Steer thought that, more to the point, he fell on his friend's feet.

With Sickert more or less as leader, the clique described by Brown planned to invite as many sympathetic artists as they could find to submit work to the NEAC jury, until eventually their circle were in the majority, and many original members resigned. And from this point Steer, however unwittingly at times, was at the centre of critical controversy for several years.

'The Most Contested Painter
of His Time'

The new spirit within the NEAC made itself more visible to the public when the nucleus around Steer, Brown and Sickert exhibited as 'The London Impressionists' at the Goupil Gallery in December 1889. Having deliberately chosen the title, they then attempted to play down its significance to the press. Sickert commented that Impressionist was simply a label that the press would give them. Given the usual glib identification of any work that could conceivably be associated with any French influence, or which appeared at all strange, his comment was no doubt to the point. It was Sickert who wrote the introduction to the catalogue of the exhibition and, echoing Whistler, he remarked that whatever Impressionism was, it was not realism: "It has no wish to record anything merely because it exists", rather, "it accepts, as the aim of the picture . . . . beauty", and as such its students studied the walls of the National Gallery, and not the "canvases that yearly line our official and unofficial shows of competitive painting" (DSM 1945 175–6). So Sickert's definition of Impressionism is more to do with a tradition of quality and trained perception than with the painterly techniques of Monet and his circle.

In general the catalogue introduction was not particularly enlightening or even especially relevant, and was dismissed as such by the Press. But, yet again, it highlights the uncertainty which surrounded definitions of Impressionism, even by the artists most clearly identified with it in England. Sickert's call for artists to express the "magic and poetry" of the streets of London did not apply to all the exhibitors, and certainly not to Steer.

Steer showed eight pictures at the Goupil Gallery and these were generally perceived in the press to be inspired by Monet. A developing interest in Monet's technique had become apparent in

Steer's painting by late 1887, and was most clearly reflected in *A Summer's Evening*, which he exhibited at the NEAC in April of the following year. This picture, which is known to have been planned and executed in his studio, was essentially an experiment with the Impressionist method. It shows three bathers, depicted in intense broken colours, thickly applied — a traditional subject but handled in a totally new manner for Steer, and not well received by some critics, as the following review suggests:

> the utter unnaturalness and audacity of Mr Wilson Steer's Summer Evening made me feel quite uncomfortable. Three nude girls with spotty orange skins, stand on a beach made of red, blue and yellow spots; the girls are in no respect even passable in appearance, the drawing imperfect and the whole composition looked to me like a piece of aggressive affectation (BL 1971 14).

A piece of criticism worthy of 'Arry Quilter himself. In his bright, freely applied colour, Steer was to depart from the sweeping tonal qualities he had adapted from Whistler and in this he was to find a method more appropriate to his sunlit scenes at the beach. Steer's constant exploration of technique, his openness to differing styles and method, is a very obvious feature of his entire career and has on occasions led to accusations that he was an overly eclectic painter with no formal language of his own. Critics constantly sought to point out similarities between Steer's work and that of other painters. *A Summer's Evening*, it was said, "looks like the work of the most extravagant and least capable of the French Impressionists" (G 1888 394).

By this stage, in the late 1880s, we have seen his developing interests range through the work of quite a large number of painters, but most notably Bastien-Lepage, Whistler, Degas, and then Monet. In this we note that Steer was most attracted to artists with a strong individual technique. It became a characteristic of his to adopt whichever approach was the most appropriate for a particular subject: in this period, for example, Whistlerian devices for portrait and studio pictures; whereas landscape or outside figure compositions, while once calling for a naturalist method, increasingly showed the influence of Monet. D.S. MacColl commented favourably on this manner of working, in an article on Steer published in *The Spectator* in 1893 entitled 'On Two

Fallacies'. He described the painter as seeking after 'Congruous Beauty', where the technique best complements the subject, as he put it, "In painting, as in literature, the poetry does not exist if the technique is not sufficient to express it" (DSM 1893 422).

A good example of Steer's appropriation of French Impressionist method to represent a classic Impressionist theme is his *Summer at Cowes*, painted on a brief visit there in 1888. The effect of sunlight on water, the bright prismatic colour and the woven brushmarks are all characteristic of Monet's own work. And yet Steer's knowledge of Monet's paintings was limited to really quite a small number. Apart from the exhibition at Dowdeswell's in June 1883, he would have most likely seen the RBA winter exhibition of 1887, which included four Monets. He may also have seen an exhibition of Monet's work in Paris in May 1887 while on a short visit.

One important source for Steer's understanding of Monet's technique was in fact John Singer Sargent. Steer had seen Sargent's *Carnation Lily, Lily Rose* at the Royal Academy in 1887 and had found it ". . . the only thing that one can care about" at that exhibition. Sargent had produced pictures with more obvious influence from Monet ever since meeting and painting with him at Giverny in 1887. Sargent joined the NEAC in 1888 — he and Steer became good friends and were not unalike in character. Both were generally unassuming and reserved, and both, Sargent especially, were unwilling to speak in public. Sargent and his sister's flat in Carlyle Mansions was one of the few places Steer bothered to visit in later years.

In April 1889 twenty Monets were shown at an exhibition of his 'Impressions' at the Goupil, which Steer would doubtless have seen. An unsigned review appeared in *The Times* of Monet's exhibition and of the current NEAC show at the Egyptian Hall. The writer commented that although most of the NEAC members paint with pretty much the same intentions as Monet, really only Mr P.W. Steer and Mr John Sargent were as "marvellous in their choice of colours". Monet himself was described as an "extremely original painter", yet one who would "severely strain the faith of the ordinary British visitor" (T 1889 8).

It would be true to say that by 1889 a sympathetic response to Monet was beginning to emerge from some quarters of the Press, even though the large majority of critics and public remained hostile. From these reactions similar to that provoked by Steer's own *A Summer's Evening* were not uncommon. One critic, writing of Monet's exhibition, acknowledged the general failure of appreciation to such an extent that he even advised his readers on how to actually look at the works; that if they kept two-thirds of the width of the gallery between themselves and the canvas, then they might begin to appreciate how charming was the landscape before them. The prejudiced and ill-informed tenor of most criticism of the Impressionists meant that, on the whole, their defence was left to those critics who supported NEAC artists like Steer from the early 1890s — writers like MacColl, Stevenson and Moore.

Of those eight pictures which Steer showed at the London Impressionists, one at least was beyond the powers of apprehension of his staunchest ally later — D.S. MacColl — and illustrates just how quickly he progressed through a range of innovative influences in those years.

The picture in question was *Knucklebones*, and was painted during Steer's visit with Fred Brown to Walberswick probably earlier in 1889. It shows a group of children playing on the pebbly beach, with, as Sickert later observed, that spirit of childlike innocence and unselfconsciousness that was common in his Walberswick period. There has been much debate as to where the exact stylistic influences lay for this; a sophisticated understanding of Monet, or an experiment in the neo-Impressionist technique of Seurat.

MacColl's response highlights some of the prejudice in his attitudes to his friend's work which would become more apparent in subsequent years. MacColl noted that *Knucklebones*, with the broken texture of the handling of the shingle, had been mistaken for an "exercise in Seurat's pointillisme" — the method by which dots of primary colours mix in the eye of the spectator to create brighter secondary colours, thereby giving an intense effect at a distance. MacColl rejected this method and felt that Seurat himself had "ruined a fine original sense of colour by substituting the ridiculous shower of dots" (DSM 1945 37).

Clearly then he would not wish to see Steer experimenting with the same procedure, and so he rejected the picture as "actually a Pre-Raphaelite-like rendering of the pebbles" (ibid). Not a convincing argument, and in reality his own theory of Steer's search for 'congruous beauty' would have had more relevance — Steer choosing a method that seemed to best approximate the subject, using colour division for the shingle beach, and Monet's brushstrokes for the sea.

It was for paintings like *Knucklebones* that Steer came to be regarded as the most successful follower of Monet within the nucleus of the NEAC. As Fred Brown wrote, Steer's art was in those days "a sort of standard around which the stiffest fighting took place". But, as Brown also mentions, Steer himself took little interest in the political questions which arose and was "more amused than interested" at the various meetings that took place (FB 1930 277).

In spite of the increased acclaim he received from his friends, the general level of public opinion over his work continued to be uncomplimentary. For popular art criticism, association with French Impressionism, and with Monet in particular, was not to be encouraged. It was the work of Steer and Sickert which seemed to turn the critics against the Goupil exhibition as a whole, even though they had only fourteen works between them in a show of seventy paintings. A writer in the *Graphic* stated that Steer's "Monet-inspired canvases reflect the most objectionable peculiarities of the same painter's method". He went on to comment that some of the pictures in that exhibition were "remarkable only for their eccentricity and bizarre extravagance" (G 1889 702). Impressionism in the eyes of this writer and of the wider public continued to be a general label for any form of painting that appeared new or different. The critic in the *Illustrated News* regarded the "crude colouring, grotesque posturing . . . . and alarming perspective" of French inspired works as a "travesty of nature" (IN 1889 724).

So from this viewpoint, far from setting the standard as Brown and his colleagues felt, to the general public Steer and Sickert were responsible for the notoriety of the NEAC. This only serves to illustrate the continuing narrow-mindedness towards contemporary French art as late as 1889.

The tone of the critical attacks on Steer and his work often seem to be describing some wild-eyed, violent extremist with little sense of public decency. An absurd view when placed in the context of memories of his character. William Rothenstein recalled a man with the "conservative instincts and prejudices of the middle class Englishman", and a "stolid unimaginativeness" (WR 1931 170).

Yet by 1889 a measure of international recognition had arisen for Steer, which must have helped to lift his spirits, when he was invited to take part in the February exhibition of Les XX in Brussels. He showed five pictures at this exhibition, including *The Bridge*, then owned by Sickert, and *A Summer's Evening*. These works were hung alongside paintings by Seurat, Pissarro and Gauguin, and were generally well received by the Belgian Press. Les XX was a secessionist group of artists with Art Nouveau and Symbolist affiliations, which had formed in 1884 with an aim not dissimilar to that of the NEAC — to provide a forum for younger artists. Each year the group chose an additional twenty artists to show with them in their February exhibition. Mainly French artists were chosen, for "their distinction and/or avant-gardism". Of artists from Britain Whistler and Sickert were the most notable representatives.

Steer's seaside Impressionist paintings of the coasts of Northern France and Suffolk continued for a couple of years into the 1890s. One of the most vivid examples is *Boulogne Sands*, 1889–90, where again the technical style echoes both Monet and Seurat. The scene is of children digging sandcastles on a beach lined with striped bathers huts. As in all of the pictures concerned with this theme it is the representation of the bright noonday sunlight that preoccupies Steer. The brilliant impressionism of his work conveys the glare of the full sun with vibrant colour, rapid brushstrokes and summarily drawn figures.

This particular work was not exhibited until 1892, possibly because Steer knew it would have a bad general response. It was D.S. MacColl in his review in *The Spectator* who gave the most positive account of the work:

> *Boulogne Sands* is the very music of colour in its gayest and most singing moments, and every character and association of the scene helps by suggestion in the merry fete of light . . . (DSM 1945 45).

He went on to describe the elements of the scene, which he likened to the "sharp notes of pipes and strings sounding to an invitation by Ariel", and then remarked that despite all this, "nine out of ten people will get no further than to notice that one of the little girls has awkward legs . . ."

It was possibly as a result of the kind of stubborn and unsophisticated criticism that MacColl mentions, that Steer began in 1889 to produce a series of portraits and interior figure studies which were to prove more popular with the public and were stylistically much more moderate. The model for the majority of these portraits was Rose Pettigrew, whose relationship with Steer lasted until around 1895, and which seems to have been the only significant romantic involvement of Steer's life. The single substantial account of this was produced by Pettigrew herself in the mid nineteen-forties. Interestingly the affair, which was doubtless of great importance to Steer, is never mentioned in writings on him by friends and associates.

Pettigrew recounts meeting Steer at the age of twelve, having been taken with her family to London after her father's death. She and her sisters were first engaged as models by Millais, an arrangement which lasted for several apparently glorious weeks. From then on the three sisters posed for numerous artists, particularly Whistler, but also including Poynter, Leighton, Holman Hunt and Sargent — they were "the rage among the artists". It is worth noting that her account gushes in this vein throughout. The enormous conceit and self-obsession evident in Rose Pettigrew's writing does make it appear highly questionable, or at best tinged with no small measure of fantasy.

Steer took her on as a model, to the annoyance of Whistler, and without knowing her real age. She describes how fond she was of Steer, and of how he monopolised her time as a model. Yet she points out his meanness towards her — how he only gave her three presents in all the time she knew him, and that she posed for him for practically no money because she wanted to help him and didn't realise how financially secure he was in reality. Nevertheless she loved him, she claims. But later she returned his ring, knowing that they could never live together happily, so possibly the two had become engaged. If so she could have been little more than eighteen or nineteen at the end of their relationship, and Steer was in his mid-thirties.

The earliest picture we have of her is *The Sofa*, painted in 1889, when she must have been thirteen. She poses, reading on the sofa in front of the drawn curtains of Steer's new studio in Maclise Mansions in Addison Road. Essentially the picture is composed from large contrasting masses of light and dark — the curtains, the lighter fabric of the sofa, and the darkness of the dress. *The Sofa*, when exhibited that year, was certainly rather more popular with critics than much of his work to date. Viewed as one of the most "challenging canvases" in the exhibition, one critic summed up the picture "as a piece of decoration in the strictest sense of the word, it is acceptable" (MA 1889 24). But the most successful of these early works is *Jonquils*, of 1890. A half-length profile, again against the window with a similar interest in contrasting light and shade but rather more sensitively handled than the previous picture.

It was at this point, in 1890, that MacColl first got to know Steer personally, having spent the previous early years of the NEAC travelling and lecturing, and now succeeding Harry Quilter as art critic of *The Spectator*. The painting *Jonquils* was shown at the NEAC in April, and MacColl commented on it in his review, regarding it as the best picture in the exhibition. *Jonquils* was also one of the first of Steer's paintings to be sold for a reasonable price. It was bought for forty-five pounds by William Burrell who had been taken to his studio by John Lavery.

Figure painting was in general more favourably received than landscapes, even in the early 1890s — one factor perhaps in the public appeal of *Jonquils*. MacColl felt Steer was more successful in this respect:

> Visitors to last years exhibition will remember Mr Steer's experimental work with its strongly worked scheme of colour . . . . this year it seems to us Mr Steer has not only tried, but has eminently succeeded. The design has invention but also restfulness and simplicity, that comes of completed invention (DSM 1890 478).

For Steer, landscape and outside figure studies offered more scope for experimentation than portraits. Or at least technically the subject called for the loosely handled approach of Impressionism. Portraits, though, seem to have required something more approaching the Whistlerian technique with restricted colour and emphasis on tone and overall design. This less adventurous handling was clearly more appealing to the public, and in this instance to MacColl as well.

From 1890 MacColl became the most outspoken supporter of Steer. From this time his critical utterances in effect shaped public perceptions of the painter's work. The two developed a friendship which lasted until Steer's death. Although at times he found MacColl's intellectual rigour rather hard going, Steer generally had great respect for his opinions, and maintained that he was the finest critic of modern painting of his time, and had "thought the matter out", as he put it.

MacColl was a Scot, born in Glasgow in 1859. Originally intended for the Church, he went to Oxford to study Latin and Greek, but by the early 1890s he was a student at Fred Brown's studio at Westminster, where Henry Tonks, another of Steer's circle, had also studied. His appointment as art critic of *The Spectator* coincided with George Moore's at *The Speaker*, and so from the beginning of the 1890s Steer's work was discussed in public in more serious and generally positive terms than previously. The phenomenon of MacColl joining the staff at *The Spectator* is interesting in itself, and is of relevance for several reasons. It meant that the NEAC finally had a voice within the Press, which would ultimately lead to greater acceptance, and in Steer's case in particular, to wider recognition. Initially though the appointments caused much disruption and led to often hostile critical debate raging from one journal to another.

Alfred Thornton was astounded that the solid and solemn *Spectator* should have taken on such a "revolutionary art critic". Moreover, he added, this "terrible man" wrote uncommonly well; there was both style and sting in his articles, which hurt quite as much as, possibly even more than, the able but rougher contributions of George Moore (AT 1938 20). MacColl himself admitted to his surprise at being offered his new post, and commented later that it gave him a remarkable opportunity: "as if a heretic had been offered the pulpit of St Paul's" (DSM 1945 43). The emergence in the primarily conservative press of a group of critics who were sympathetic to more radical artists, as Steer was perceived to be, forms part of the shift in outlook, the transition in culture that characterises the last decade of the nineteenth century.

MacColl, along with Moore and other critics such as R.A.M. Stevenson, were involved in more direct and individual forms of writing, and with a diversity of attitudes and beliefs which, by the 1890s, were commonly accepted as the 'New Journalism'. From the standpoint of the proprietors of journals and newspapers, the new direction of the press was partly a search for a wider readership. There was a new emphasis on lively debate, on combating monotony, and a move away from the dull fastidiousness of much recent journalism. A programme not unlike that of the painters at the New English Art Club.

The American method of signing articles was adopted, giving writers more personal responsibility for their work, and encouraging greater thought and originality. Therefore articles contained 'views, not news', they were more critical and less purely descriptive. This was envisaged as a departure from the standard journalism of previous years. One editor typical of this old style informed a colleague that he "did not want an excellent writer, still less a thinker. I want a man who can put commonplace ideas into pompous English" (HM 1898 217).

And this was a fairly apt description of several of the early commentators on Steer; of 'Arry, in particular. So there was an underlying desire in the 1890s to raise standards of debate and levels of taste. There is a sense of ambivalence here: on the one hand a wish to improve the intellectual climate; and on the other to attract more readers. And, more peculiarly still for financial concerns, an almost anti-commercial stance that was similarly reflected among the membership of the NEAC — Steer perhaps especially.

The educational ambitions of these journals were taken seriously by the likes of MacColl, who maintained a fairly low opinion of their readers' powers of perception. Both he and Moore tended to treat the public 'like a bumpkin'. They also used their columns as invaluable platforms from which to continue their denouncement of institutions like the Royal Academy, very much in the wake of Whistler. For Moore in particular, space was provided to continue his attack on the philistine elements of the middle classes and on mediocrity in general. There was room for greater display of wit — the cult of the personality was as central to the press as it was to the arts in the 1890s — from, for example, Wilde, Whistler and Walter

Sickert. The latter particularly enjoyed the scope that the Press allowed him to express his views.

A large section of the 'New' Press was given over to criticism of general opinion and accepted taste. In this the terms 'middle class' and 'mediocre' were synonymous. Many 'New' journalists felt that they were out to conquer mediocrity — which was the sanctuary of the philistine. The dissemination and ultimate acceptance of new ways of looking at art and morality were unattainable so long as philistinism was dominant.

Osbert Sitwell gave a good account of the strength of philistine ideology: "We had been taught to avoid the society of anyone intelligent, and to shun the creative . . . . as though they conveyed to others some hideous infection" (OS 1947 xiii).

From after the turn of the century this anti-philistinism led to a widespread interest in Nietzsche's writings amongst these circles, and Nietzschean pretensions abounded. Steer, of course, could never be accused of those. Sickert's editor at the *New Age* — A.R. Orage — quoted Nietzsche in his journal: "The secret of a joyful life is to live dangerously." Steer certainly never did that. Contemporary accounts of Steer present an image of a man quite at odds with this ideal. William Rothenstein, in his recollections, remembers that one of Steer's few comments on literary criticism was that he "didn't see why anyone need write poetry now, wasn't Byron good enough?" His political views were equally conservative:

> Had he been a politician he would have voted against the Reform Bill, against the abolition of the army purchase system, against the entry of Jews and Roman Catholics in the House of Commons. Why change? He would have said; change only means bother and England is all right as she is (WR 1931 170).

This attitude infuriated friends and colleagues from time to time. Rothenstein also considered that in his passion for collecting Chelsea figures, Steer displayed the "best bad taste" of anyone he knew. But for all this conservatism, the intellectual sloth and the unadventurous lifestyle that the painter has been accused of, there was one factor in Steer that guaranteed support from Moore et al — his pictures. For Rothenstein, he was a revolutionary painter who hated change.

Critics saw great potential in Steer's work in the 1890s. As MacColl put it: "Mr Steer has not, or has not yet, the science in singing of a Manet, but at least he has a voice" (SR 1896 621–2). And George Moore, in characteristically egotistical fashion, boasted that on arrival in London Steer was the painter who he had "the wit to pick out as one who could replace the gap made in my life by the absence of Manet" (GM 1930 99).

Moore, while for the most part regarded affectionately by his friends, was at times outrageously ill-informed in his writings and often prone to these self-aggrandisements. Having studied art in Paris in 1873 he had some brief acquaintance with Manet and the Impressionists around the end of that decade. By the time of his arrival in London he had embroidered this acquaintance considerably and dined out on tales of his intimate relationship with Manet. This was much to the amusement of his circle in later years, especially to Sickert, who cherished Moore's comments on art as so much sublime nonsense. Steer was similarly tickled by his more absurd pretensions. However, despite the cant, and the fact that many of the views he expressed were stolen from other sources, he was nevertheless an entertaining critic of the cultural conditions of the time, and was certainly useful in his support for those artists that he considered to have stepped out of the morass of philistine virtues — Steer included. His espousal of the dominant figures at the NEAC in fact gave shape and substance to his critical dilettantism.

For Moore and MacColl, appreciation of Steer was a virtual act of connoisseurship, and MacColl in particular went to great lengths to persuade the public of the intrinsic value of his work. In this also he was helped by the new atmosphere of serious consideration that the journals were encouraging. For the most part, previous exhibition reviews had consisted of little more than lists of painters' names, with perhaps a brief, one-line description of the subject matter of their work. According to George Moore, reviews of this type had more of the appearance of an advertisement than an intelligent attempt at real discussion on the merits or demerits of a painting. Moore used the opportunity to make an attack on art dealers, for whom the Press was "a dupe". He claimed that "These notices taken out in the form of legitimate advertising would run into hundreds of pounds" (GM 1893 154–5).

These short notices were sometimes the result of sheer lack of time, a hurried glance around the gallery walls, and off to the next show. Sickert satirized those writers' attitudes:

A critic, bored and sick to death of pictures, comes to our work. Oh, so-and-so! What on earth can I say? Oh! 'Serious effort and probity of vision!' That will have to do (OS 1947 58).

The 'New Critics', as they were soon to be described, had more time to construct their articles, as well as more freedom in the choice of which exhibitions to review. Critics of the old school, when dealing with a subject at length, tended to be turgid and diffuse. Their writing was commonly based almost exclusively on the subject matter of a painting — its associations and its sentiments. This was especially so in the case of critics who were not themselves painters. And it should be noted that many of the 'new critics' — MacColl, R.A.M. Stevenson, C.J. Holmes, and slightly later, Roger Fry — all painted seriously. This gave them greater insight and interest in technical matters.

These new critics rejected the pseudo-moral concerns of previous criticism. One of the most important influences for MacColl in that respect were the opinions on art of Whistler — the belief that art had no concern with anything outside of itself. MacColl shared the view of the artist as autonomous and uncompromised by external conditions. There lay the foundations of Formalist criticism that would be built upon by Fry. MacColl's own painterly ideals and those of the painters he most admired led to an almost exclusive attention to the intrinsic properties of the paint and the method of its application. Ideally subject matter was arbitrary; it was a simple motive for transporting paint onto canvas, and the completed work was to be evaluated through its overall pictorial qualities, its design and organisation. In this framework, any discussion of the sentiment of the picture, or the authenticity of detail, was irrelevant. Any critic who wanted to encourage sound painting must insist on a thorough understanding of the medium itself. It was in this context — the skill and craftsmanship of his painting — that MacColl saw the value of Steer. In effect then, Steer was a painter's painter.

But this approach, the form of criticism which MacColl pursued in his writing throughout the 1890s and 1900s, was a far cry from conventional criticism. The 'New Critics' received as much, if not more, hostile abuse from reactionary quarters as did the painters that they supported.

MacColl played a lively part in the tirade against the 'Philistine' during these years — by which he identified the average exhibition-goer, the Royal Academy and its pictures, its critical supporters and its collecting policies. The battle between the philistine and the new critic was waged from column to column, and was just the kind of verbal scuffle that the editors hoped for.

One such altercation began when in 1892 an article appeared in the *Pall Mall Gazette*, which rejected the work of both the 'New Critics' and 'New Painters', and claimed that the unpopularity of those artists lay in their contempt for the importance of subject. "What the British public wants", the writer declared, "is pictures of dogs and babies, of Granny's chairs and Mother's darling, of moving tales by flood and field" (AT 1938 21).

MacColl argued that it was not the business of painters or critics to simply give the public what it wants. Nor could the artist depict a subject which he or she knew would be acceptable, and yet "treat it artistically", for in doing so, "the popularity would be seen to have vanished."

The most often cited example of these battles within the press was the outcry that resulted from the exhibition of Degas' *L'Absinthe* at the International Society show at the Grafton Galleries at the beginning of 1893. The 'Philistine' speaking from the columns of the Westminster Gazette found it hilarious that MacColl should have deemed such a repulsive subject as "two rather sodden people drinking in a cafe" to be "mysterious", "affecting" and to "set a standard" of beauty, decorativeness and skill (WG 1893 232). A clear example of the antithetical positions of the two critics: for one, subject is paramount, for the other the use of paint, the handling, is everything. The Philistine, like 'Arry, was happy to be considered as one of the 'populace' and for MacColl, the affliction was incurable, 'Arry would never understand the true value of painting, and as MacColl put it, he even regarded Mr Steer as "too good and able to paint as he did".

Despite his negative views of the public's powers of apprehension, MacColl did endeavour to explain the aims of Impressionist art in clear and concise terms. He tried to show that an Impressionist picture was not a hastily conceived and executed sketch, and that Impressionism was not a fad, but that a true understanding of Impressionism would reveal its firm traditional and historical antecedents.

These views were expressed to an extent by Steer himself in what was for him a unique lecture, which he was invited to give to the Art Workers' Guild in 1891. The Guild had been absorbed by the Arts and Crafts Exhibition Society in 1888. It was their aesthetic programme that Sickert had criticised in the introduction to the London Impressionists. Walter Crane was a leading light in the Guild and his reactions to the controversy around *L'Absinthe* were later noted by George Moore. Crane had regarded the painting as fit only for an "illustrated tract in temperance propaganda" and as a "study of human degradation" (GM 1893 269).

Given the general opinion of the Guild's members it must have been with some trepidation that Steer stood to deliver himself on the subject of 'Impressionism in Art'. And his repeated emphasis on the importance of tradition in Impressionism was no doubt partly stressed in order to reassure his audience:

> I have both read and heard it stated that Impressionists ignore tradition. Now, I propose to show that so far from ignoring tradition they follow the highest tradition of all time which is inspired by nature and nature only.
>
> Impressionism is not a new thing created by this generation. The word is new, I grant, and herein lies the trouble. Everyone seems to put his own construction on the word. For the sake of simplicity, let us substitute the word Art for Impressionism — there can be only two things, Art or no Art. I think the definition which someone has given that art is the expression of an impression seen through a personality sums up the question as to what art is very concisely.

Steer at this point proposed to read extracts from the discourses of Sir Joshua Reynolds, whom he regarded as an Impressionist and whose views he felt were precisely the same as those of the Impressionists of his own day. And he asked:

> Is it a craze that we should recognise the fact that nature is bathed in atmosphere? Is it a fashion to treat a picture so that unity of vision may be achieved by insisting on certain parts more than others? No! It is not a fashion, it is a *law*.

He then remarked on those pictures painted currently which were popular and sold for high prices and which were singularly lacking in this all-important "unity of vision". All so laboriously detailed that:

> with these tiresome exercises of misguided industry you may make six pictures out of one and each is as finished and as badly composed as the others.

In words which echoed those of Sickert's earlier preface, he went on:

> The Impressionist is inspired by his own time because his art is inspired by nature; he finds his pictures in the scenes around him,

but using the best principles that have informed the production of great art in all time. There followed a list of those artists who by Steer's definition could be characterised as Impressionists. These included Giotto, Veronese, Velazquez and Gainsborough. So, he continued:

> Impressionism is of no country and of no period, it has been from the beginning; it bears the same relation to painting that poetry does to journalism. Two men paint the same model; one creates a poem, the other is satisfied with recording facts.

In his final paragraph he concluded that art must be progressive. It is not enough to keep repeating the work of painters from previous generations however admirable it might be, even if in some cases that might be a popular and financially successful occupation, and, as he ends:

> It has always been the case in the history of Art that the men who are trying to add something to the sum of what has already been achieved meet with opprobrium and scorn at the hands of the multitude (DSM 1945 177–8).

No mention whatsoever of the French Impressionists, of Monet or Degas, which was probably diplomatic in the face of his audience. However, in his reference to those highly finished and overly detailed pictures of the popular Academicians, he may have been interpreted as attacking also the Pre-Raphaelite painters whose influence continued to be felt within the Arts and Crafts Society.

This citing of Velazquez and Gainsborough as Impressionists, in his sense, is interesting in the context of the concerns of his fellow critics; and with Gainsborough in particular, in relation to his own later work. His assertion that art should progress and not simply re-echo past styles is also relevant, in the light of his own work, given that this objection was often raised about his own painting of subsequent years.

The final comment on the treatment of the progressive artist from the mass of public opinion is typical of remarks made by MacColl and Moore. It is particularly a defence of his own position at the time, and against the attacks he still received. The stress on the importance of a 'unity of vision', where certain parts of a picture are treated with more emphasis than others, was analogous to Whistler's views, and was also important to MacColl and to the writings of R.A.M. Stevenson. For example, MacColl admired the selection of detail and the effect of arrangement in Steer's portraits of Pettigrew. And the insistence on the importance of poetry — that "Impressionism is to art as poetry is to journalism" — resounds throughout so much 'advanced' critical opinion of the time.

Like Steer, MacColl identified Impressionism as dealing with universal principles in art — in his view, with 'truth'. In his review of the spring exhibition of the NEAC in 1891 he observed this concern with truth: "that is to a refined vision of the object". Here he distinguished the work of the English painters from the Impressionists of the French school, from their "effort to catch and render fleeting and transitory things that will not sit . . ." (DSM 1891 544).

In spite of a perceptive understanding of Monet's paintings, and an appreciation of his early works in particular, MacColl had more sympathy for Manet and for Degas. This predilection is felt in his writing on Steer — the fact that he had a greater affinity for the portraits, with their concern for form and overall composition, rather than with the more Monet/Seurat-influenced landscapes and outside figure studies. The former embodied to a larger extent that concept of a unity of vision, in MacColl's view, and demonstrated more concern for selectivity. The importance of selectivity is constantly emphasised, and it was the inability of the Academic painter to select from nature that he underlined in his article on 'Painting and Imitation' in 1892. The painter, he said, "went out to fish and comes vaguely home with a bucket of water" (DSM 1931 196). Fundamental to this selective approach was the ability to draw. Drawing, for him, was a kind of gesture. Steer was often criticised for his lack of skill as a draughtsman — although MacColl rejected this — and he claimed anyway that it is "the verve of the performance, not the closeness of the imitation that impresses". For MacColl Degas was the "greatest living virtuoso of drawing" (DSM 1898 426), with a sense of formal beauty and vital structure, and he detected a similar "trenchancy of drawing" in Manet.

However, MacColl's desire to site Steer's art in relation to the art of Manet and Degas rather than Monet or Pissarro was not shared by all. One notable exception to MacColl's judgement was the response to Steer by Camille Pissarro's son Lucien, who was staying in London at this time and who also spoke at the Art Workers' Guild meeting in 1891. Lucien and Steer seem to have struck a brief but immediate friendship and Lucien was more favourably impressed by his work than by any of the other 'English Impressionists', including Sickert, whose work he described as "Deplorable!" Of Steer he wrote in a letter to his father:

> He divides his tones as we do and is very intelligent; here is a real artist! However he has doubts because the others laugh at him and no-one understands him. We will become close friends, I think. He has the air of being very happy to make my acquaintance and tells me that he prefers your work to Monet's (J. Rewald 1950 25).

That the friendship was never established further was possibly due to the language difficulties that both artists faced, and possibly also because the 'division of tones' that Lucien referred to — the exercises in neo-Impressionism which Steer had carried out just prior to their meeting — were not maintained. Doubtless MacColl's lack of sympathy in that area had some effect on Steer.

It is clear then that around the beginning of the 1890s there was a considerable mix of opinion, even among his close friends, as to the position of Steer's art — whether his works should be viewed as innovative and in line with recent developments in French art, or if he should be considered a traditionalist upholding universal principles. Walter Sickert's remarks on Steer from this time emphasise that confusion, and seek to place him apart from it:

> The painter is not, fortunately for his enduring reputation, dans le mouvement. If his work is not to be considered old-fashioned, it is because he has never been new-fangled. He is not, Dieu Merci, 'up to date', or vingtième siecle, or nouveau salon. He is not a decadent, nor a symbolist, nor a Rosicrucian. It is impossible to fit him into any of the labels of chic journalism. He belongs to no local or temporary school . . . And yet he contrives to interest us . . . (WS 1893 223).

These difficulties in categorisation were created partly as a result of the way his allies — MacColl especially — struggled to identify him with their own aesthetic ideals, and partly also due to the constantly diverse styles which Steer adopted around this time. A diversity that would only increase in subsequent years.

In 1891–2 Steer was still absorbed by the influence of Monet and to an extent by neo-Impressionism, with his use of broken dabs of colour. These can be seen most effectively in several of his yacht paintings produced from a trip to Cowes in the summer of 1892. But in two of his figure paintings from around this time we can still see the influences of both Whistler and Degas.

Steer's painting of *Mrs Cyprian Williams and Her Two Little Girls*, now in the Tate Gallery, is of interest here. This portrait was commissioned by Francis James, a watercolourist and member of the London Impressionists group. The subject was an artist herself and was exhibiting at the NEAC in 1891–2. She was also the wife of the collector T. Cyprian Williams, and was apparently well-known for her bad temper, which the piercing expression on her face clearly reflects. The most immediate aspect of the picture is the striking perspective, looking down on the central figure in a strong diagonal composition. This echoed, albeit rather uneasily, the bizarre compositional arrangements of Degas, and was used again by Steer in his *Prima Ballerina Assoluta*, exhibited at the NEAC at the same time in August 1891. MacColl noted the influence of Degas, the strange effect of cropping which occurred with photography, and the bearing that the huge fashion for Japanese prints had on these paintings. (In his role as avid collector, Steer was the owner of a group of nineteenth century Japanese prints, including, most notably, work by Utamaro.) The most successful aspect of the *Mrs Cyprian Williams* portrait grouping is the treatment of the two children. Their carefree self-possession and awkwardness is reminiscent of his representations of children playing on the beach in *Boulogne Sands* or *Knucklebones*, and in stark opposition to the stern profile of their mother.

Another interesting portrait of this period is *The Blue Dress*, 1892. The model, Rose Pettigrew, is seated stiffly in front of a darkened window and casts a strong shadow to the left of the picture. Her slight hands, very sensitively drawn, stretch across her knee, and the overall atmosphere is composed and graceful. The full title of the picture when exhibited (translated from the Latin) reads: "My soft heart is always liable to injury by light weapons. And the perpetual reason is that I am always in love". MacColl described the picture in *The Spectator* (1892) and made comparisons with Romney: ". . . But Romney's colour would look cheap beside this and his drawing conventional in observation however big in style" (DSM 1945 44).

He stressed the "excellence of drawing" together with the "loveliness of colour" as a snub to those who often felt Steer's drawing to be inadequate. He observed a "look of scarcely arrested life, of movement caught in passage", noticed the subtle touches of reflected colour, and regarded it as a wholly successful work uniting so many qualities. George Moore rejected MacColl's review thereby sparking off a brief altercation between *The Spectator* and *The Speaker*. Steer, blithely engrossed in his painting and his relationship with Rose, had inadvertently initiated yet another warring of words. Moore suggested that Watts was a more likely comparison than Romney, and criticised the drawing, feeling the whole work lacked atmosphere in the handling.

Steer's visit to Cowes that summer had been particularly productive and resulted in a series of pictures of the yachts which reflected a range of stylistic explorations. The environment at Cowes in full sunshine was a perfect setting for an artist with the example of Monet or Seurat in mind. Some of the paintings are exercises in the technique of Seurat, and others of Monet. George Moore also noted this in Whistler's *Two Yachts*, in the treatment of light and rigging in twilight. There had been a retrospective exhibition of Whistler at the Goupil Gallery in March which would have revived Steer's interest before setting out on his trip.

In *Procession of Yachts at Cowes* the closeness of the yacht and its masts divides the canvas into grid-like proportions. Bands of horizontals and verticals contrast with the billowing sweep of the sails in the background, making a striking compositional effect. The white sails contain reflections of lilac and grey, and the paint is thickly applied. MacColl felt that, unlike the earlier *Knucklebones*, he could see direct evidence of Seurat and Pissarro's influence here. But he said this grudgingly — it was only in the "distantly allied technique", and Steer only used broken touches of colour and stayed clear of the dreaded dots (DSM 1945 37–8).

Moore however recalled visiting an exhibition of paintings by Seurat and Pissarro in Paris in 1881–2 (in fact his memory was playing tricks — the event in question was the Impressionist exhibition in 1886). Ten of the works were pictures of yachts in full sail, all painted in clear tints with no atmospheric effects and in a series of little dots. The similarity to Steer's pictures is striking, but MacColl made little of the connection, so opposed was he to the *pointilliste* technique in general, and to Steer's experiments with it in particular.

II

1893–1909

Traditional Values

In 1892 Brown, who was still teaching at the Westminster school, was appointed Slade Professor after Legros' resignation. Brown was chosen in preference to two Academicians, apparently because it was felt that he was more likely to make a success of the School. This in itself was a sign of the more general disillusionment with the Academy and its standards of training in the early 1890s. One writer applauded Brown's election to the post on the grounds that a school of painting "on the advanced lines of the thought of the day" might mean that "those who desire a more unconventional training should not be driven to France to study" (MA 1893 216).

Soon afterwards Brown invited Henry Tonks to be his assistant. Tonks had originally studied medicine, and at the time of his appointment to the Slade he was a demonstrator in anatomy at the London Hospital Medical School, a position he apparently loathed. His drawing had developed as an all-consuming passion while he was a medical student, and he was always able to draw from the dead, at least. As a medical officer at the Royal Free Hospital Tonks had attended Brown's evening classes at Westminster. At the same time David Muirhead and Steer's friend Ronald Gray were also studying there.

Tonks's interests in art soon outweighed his interests in medicine, and gradually he arranged his hospital business to fit in with his evening classes. He credited Brown with great skill at teaching the principles of drawing, which he could combine with his own knowledge of anatomy. Tonks described the Westminster School as a "truly comic and dirty little studio" which nevertheless became a powerful centre of reaction against the established institutions of the day (HT 1929 230).

It was at about this time that Ronald Gray introduced Tonks to Steer. He remembered Steer as a tall man, comparatively thin, and

59

with a slightly melancholy outlook. In 1893 Brown appointed Steer to teach painting one day a week at the Slade. The original plan was for him to teach until his own work was successful enough to support him alone. These three formed a trio who were to have a strong influence on the reputation of the Slade, and on the early careers of many students up to the First World War, and after in the case of Steer and Tonks. Their teaching skills were remembered with praise by some, although their personalities, set against each other, seemed eccentric and mildly comic as the years passed. Caricatures by illustrators such as Max Beerbohm and E. Heber Thompson present Tonks as lanky and stooped with a fearsome expression, and Steer increasingly rotund and placid. This physical contrast was borne out in their characters. Students recalled Tonks' ferocious criticisms and sharp sarcasm, whereas Steer was ever mild and pacifying, often consoling students who had suffered too much from the rudeness of Tonks's remarks. Tonks did not hesitate in telling aspiring artists they were hopelessly untalented. In one famous instance he told a young woman student to stop wasting her time and get back to her needlework. Steer's response to such situations was a pat on the knee and later an encouraging remark on their work.

It is ironic in fact that after the turn of the century, when equality for women became an increasingly debated topic, that the Slade School, with around seventy per cent female students, should have been led by three such confirmed bachelors. One — namely Tonks — was a virtual misogynist, and all three were apparently quite ignorant of the issues that concerned women at that time. Tonks was renowned for making scathing comments to women students and generally judged what he viewed as feminine characteristics of their work to be incompatible with quality in art. His consistent disparagement is without doubt one factor in the explanation of why so many of those women abandoned their careers at such an early age, or else shifted to areas in art where they could keep their distance from him. In some instances Tonks' character even put off women from joining the Slade at all. Stella Bowen recorded going to an interview there and being "completely crushed by the aspect of the Professor who received me. I don't know whether it was the famous Tonks or the famous Brown, but he was eight feet tall and conceived it as his duty to put the fear of God into me". Instead she took herself to the Westminster School where "they didn't believe in grief and tears [and] never had any suicides amongst the students" (SB 1924 45). In such circumstances it is clear that Steer, by contrast, would be regarded with affection, even if a few of his students — Dorothy Brett for example — found him a bad teacher because he said so little.

Steer's method of teaching was, as one would expect, to instruct by example. Appearing behind a student, taking the brush, making a few marks and moving on. His most constructive verbal comments would be to tell the student to "go on with that" or to say that a particular sketch or picture had "come off". This was a phrase he often used with regard to his own work — the sense that something was right and worth continuing, or wasn't and should be left. In a conversation with the editor of *The Artist* Steer commented that he held no dogmatic views as to what students should do — there was no one and only method to be adopted. He realised, he said, that "all must work out their own redemption" (TA 1933 149).

Steer was not noted for his concern with teaching drawing, and would leave that issue aside. Since the time of Legros drawing had been one of the most important aspects of training at the Slade, and was obviously of paramount importance to Tonks, and also to Brown. One ex-student later recalled Steer's attitude:

> Steer did not see in line. At the Slade School in the nineties, when under the influence of Fred Brown and Henry Tonks, the expression of form by line was almost a cult. I once sat behind Steer as he drew a model's head for another student from the end of the semi-circle about the model's throne. The girls' head was a delicate projection from cast shadow and penumbra towards the light. Steer said, 'Why all this line? There is no line' (CA 1926 11).

Steer's interest in students working from the Antique was, again, not for the drawing, but for the practice in painting the light upon a cast. He was most noted for comments on light and also on colour. With colour he dealt instinctively, and told one of his students: "A picture has to be nice colour from beginning to end" (DSM 1945 134). He would stress the importance of using the correct brushes in this context, rejecting the square cut brushes that had been so popular with the rustic naturalists, in favour of small round ones which could deal more effectively with gradations of colour. One student was told: "You will never become a colourist without small round brushes". And the brushes were held lightly, the colour to be laid "like a breath".

Tonks, quite unlike Steer, was renowned for his volubility on art, and spoke of it with a fervent religiosity that would leave Steer amused and bemused. As Tonks's biographer put it, he looked on art as the "redeeming activity of man". And although his criticisms of students were relentless, he was entirely dedicated to the Slade. He was Brown's successor in 1917, and later commented that "The Slade continues to produce geniuses, we turn them out every year" (JH 1939 58).

In his own painting Tonks was utterly fastidious. Each picture was the cause of great *angst* and torment, which led to not a little stress for his friends. As Steer said, after Tonks had finally completed a work: "Thank goodness that's off our chests". Hone recalled MacColl's view that Tonks' knowledge of all the theories of picture-making was often too visible in his own work, and he described one such as "a little epitome of painting, a history of taste". And yet Tonks, in his constant theorising, was in a sense not unlike MacColl. Together with their greater eloquence they dominated Steer, and opinion of Steer, for many years to come. Tonks in particular was described as "undeniably bigoted" and his personal antipathy to French art increased towards the end of the century. "The effect of French painting on English", he declared, "has been fatal. Fancy Shakespeare trying to write like Racine" (*Times* 1962 24).

The principles of teaching at the Slade — that constant emphasis on the importance of drawing — had firm links with much of the new criticism of the time, and its search for sound tradition and historical precedent. Drawing at the Slade was through observation and students were not concerned with producing minutely detailed copies of reality. R.A.M. Stevenson's book on Velazquez, published in 1895, became something of a bible for staff and students alike, and in its critical approach echoed many of the views of MacColl in particular.

Stevenson's emphasis on the technique and method of Velazquez' painting was found to be especially important. His stress on the relations between the forms of painting, and his use and definition of the term 'direct painting' had a special appeal for those concerned primarily with pictorial qualities and not with literary content. By 'direct painting' Stevenson expanded a method whereby each element of a work — its colour, light and shade, and the line — was treated as a unified whole. This was the complete reversal of, say, the Pre-Raphaelite method, with its working in patches and building up detail in separate parts. It was also unlike the stippling that went on at the Academy. In this respect, 'direct painting' implied the unity of vision that Steer had talked of in his Art Workers' Guild lecture. The key terms and description in Stevenson's appreciation of Velasquez had figured largely in MacColl's writings in the early 1890s. Furthermore Stevenson's discussion of the composition lines in Velasquez' *Spinners* — of the masses which "twine and interweave" in a "rhythmic and balanced pattern" — became widely used terms in the later criticism of Roger Fry, and indeed much of twentieth century formalist writing on art. Many close similarities exist between MacColl's and Stevenson's criticism. For MacColl, technique is "a condition under which the painter sees things . . . . not a mechanical beauty stuck upon the surface of a picture and detachable from it . . ." (DSM 1940 203). This in a sense implied that search for 'congruous beauty' which absorbed Steer, in MacColl's view. And for Stevenson, technique was the:

> indivisible organic body of a man's conceptions and cannot be rightly apprehended when studied in fragments (in DS 1965 81).

The emphasis in both cases is on the essential unity of approach to the act of painting. For, as MacColl continued, "You cannot define where conception leaves off and execution begins".

Another important feature of Stevenson's book was his assertion that the roots of French Impressionism lay in the Impressionist techniques of older painters like Velazquez, and their direct, unifying approach to dealing with light. In this he was speaking in the same sense as those, including Steer, who looked for the source of Impressionism in history. In terms of art criticism this concern with a linear progression of style was formalist in essence, and had developed out of recent German historical analysis and explorations of stylistic change.

But in terms of the general context of the 1890s the emphasis on tradition and the concern with history takes on a wider significance. By this time the Slade, the NEAC and the collection of critics associated with MacColl and Stevenson — for example Lawrence Binyon and Charles Holmes — were viewed in the same light by the public. The Slade was seen as a breeding ground for young NEAC exhibitors. And yet far from reflecting a unified progressive and modernist outlook, there is a sense in which a reaction against such values was taking place — something of a retrenchment, in fact. From his paintings from the latter half of the decade it can be seen that Steer himself was similarly involved in a period of reassessment.

The general adoption, by up and coming students from the Slade, of the theories and opinions on art of critics like Stevenson and MacColl, paradoxically produced a conflict between traditional values and modernist ideas about progress. The Slade, and by extension members of the NEAC, once viewed as startlingly radical by the public, were by the later 1890s recognised more as asserting the importance of established methods and techniques, combined with sound historical precedence. These institutions were viewed by growing numbers of people in a better light than the Royal Academy — and the latter survived largely through a general process of co-opting those NEAC artists whose work seemed to be the most easily accessible to its audience. Steer maintained his disinterest in the Academy's advances, partly through force of habit, a simple resistance to change rather than a firm ideological commitment. He remained loyal to the NEAC.

In February 1894 growing respect for Steer was reflected in an invitation to stage a one-man show — his first — at the Goupil Gallery in Lower Regent Street. This was one of a small yet growing number of galleries which, following the lead of the Grosvenor Gallery, had been willing to take exhibitions of work by painters who didn't necessarily already have well-established reputations. Other venues with a similar function included the Chenil Gallery and the Carfax. In contrast to the pompous grandeur of those galleries dealing with Academy pictures, these were small scale, adopting an intimate, almost domestic appearance. They suggested a quiet selectivity that was clearly not intended for those who attended more popular shows.

1. What of the War?, c.1881

2. The Swiss Alps at the
   Earls Court Exhibition,
   1887

3. The Bridge, 1887–8

4. Knucklebones, Walberswick, 1888–9

5. Girls Running, Walberswick Pier, 1891

6. The Embarkment, 1901

7.   Girl's Head in Profile, 1889

8.   Classic Landscape, 1893

9.   Richmond Castle, 1903

10. Nutting, 1905

11. The Outskirts of Montreuil, 1907

12. The River, Ironbridge, 1910

13. Dover Harbour, 1918

14. Mrs Raynes, 192.

15. Low Tide, Greenhithe, 1932

Smaller galleries like these originally had implications for the kinds of works displayed there — none of the large scale exhibition pieces of Burlington House. Instead, their works related to the size of a drawing room. Referring to the French Impressionists, Sickert had remarked that, "they made canvases . . . . such as are suitable in the rooms we live in" (OS 1947 28). And the Goupil Gallery had this pleasant, airy and relatively informal atmosphere.

The Gallery's director since 1891 was David Croal Thompson, who was at this time also editor of the *Art Journal*. He was a friend and admirer of Whistler, and had organised his retrospective in 1892. He also exhibited work by Barbizon artists such as Corot and Daubigny. Thompson was one of Steer's earliest and most significant dealers, and was one of the first to recognise the merits of the 'English Impressionists'. As a concession to one of Steer's idiosyncrasies, the walls of the gallery were hung with the heavy, deep crimson fabric usually associated with the grandiose exhibitions of established galleries such as Agnews. Steer believed pictures, his own especially, worked better with this kind of background. He heartily disliked the growing trend for using white walls, later commenting that Charles Holmes' new scheme for the National Gallery made it look like a public lavatory.

Steer exhibited forty-three paintings at the Goupil Gallery, thirty-eight of them oils and the remaining five watercolours. Generally the show was well-noticed and he received less hostile criticism than previously. R.A.M. Stevenson, writing in the *Pall Mall Gazette*, declared that:

> . . . the exhibition does much to establish Steer's credit as a painter. One of the Anglo-French school, who aims at style as well as Impressionism . . . He has been stimulated and started, as almost every man, by his forerunners (Whistler and Monet especially), but it would be wrong to say that he has not often wrestled to find a way of feeling some parts of his motifs (RAMS 1894 132).

In stating that the Anglo-French school aimed at "style as well as Impressionism", Stevenson gave added credence to the developing notion that design and arrangement were essentially British characteristics in painting. French-trained artists were commonly felt to be indifferent to composition as well as to completion. Steer possibly selected his exhibition carefully with a view to public response — his previous experiences would have encouraged him to do so. As Stevenson also remarked, the exhibition showed Steer in a more serious light than expected: "no doubt to some extent because he has wisely omitted his most doubtful and tricky experiments".

Whether or not Steer deliberately chose to leave out paintings which had caused criticism in the past, by 1894 those "doubtful and tricky experiments" with French Impressionism became less frequent and his painting began to reflect new or rediscovered sources, executed with what MacColl described as a "composing and tenacious eye" (DSM 1894 326).

MacColl was referring here to three pictures in particular. The first, *The Sofa* — the large painting of Rose Pettigrew described earlier — bought from the exhibition for 120 guineas by the designer and architect C.R. Ashbee, who was a friend of MacColl's. In this work MacColl discerned the "original living source of the painter's vision" that retained a sense of immediacy and largeness from its initial conception. The two other works in question were *Procession of Yachts* and *The Girl in Blue*. He equated the passage of masts in the painting from Cowes to music — the phrasing between intervals of bars. And in *The Girl in Blue*, he again noted Steer's skill at retaining the freshness of inspiration. It was for this very skill that Sickert, too, kept his admiration for Steer, even though differences between them were to become increasingly apparent. He wrote to him in 1895 while in Venice:

> It may be a poor compliment, but for all practical purposes the more experiences I have, the more I find that the only things that seem to me to have a direct bearing on the practical purpose of painting my pictures are the things that I have learnt from you. To see the thing all at once. To work open and loose, freely with a full brush and full colour. And to understand that when, with that full colour, the drawing has been got, the picture is done. It sounds nothing put into words, but it *is* everything put into practice (RE 1941 107).

In 1894 Steer moved from Manresa Road to a new studio in The Avenue, Fulham Road — Maclise Mansions — a dismal toplit room. His summer trips to Boulogne and Paris were the last of his French visits until 1907. This was the beginning of a period of change in Steer's life, possibly brought about by the lack of financial success his work had achieved. The support of MacColl, Stevenson and others would have encouraged a change of direction, as would the kind of critical reaction his exhibition had received. William Rothenstein recalls, in *Men and Memories*, that his studio at this point was full of unsold pictures "of yachts and the sea, and of girls with long slender legs like Sheraton tables" (WR 1932 170) — these last were the Walberswick pier paintings. Financial problems, though, were not overwhelming for Steer. Even at this stage his mother's allowance protected him from hardship. His real problem seemed to be the public disapproval for his earlier work, which made him more susceptible to the influence of his new friends.

His paintings of nudes and models in the years surrounding the Goupil show increasingly reflect an approach to painting and a range of stylistic sources more in tune with those advocated by the 'new critics'. *Girl at Her Toilet* is at the beginning of a new phase in Steer's figure painting. The most immediate reference through subject matter is to Degas. Rose wears a petticoat, one black stockinged leg across one knee, putting on her shoe. The same pose is repeated almost identically in *Self Portrait with Model* in 1894. The Degas-like composition is here elaborated even further, Steer's head is sliced off at the top of the canvas. And also with reference to Degas the colour is subdued and flat. In connection with the second picture the importance of Degas' *Woman at a Window*, 1871-2, has been observed, a painting that Sickert had owned from 1892 and with which Steer would certainly have been familiar. In this the model is seated diagonally within the format of the canvas — a tall window at her right shoulder casting light from behind. Steer used a similar device in his painting.

Degas had been mightily defended in *L'Absinthe* scandal by MacColl and Moore. Like Whistler, Degas' art was now being described as essentially classical. In the dignity and reticence of their work, and in their handling of the problem of colour, similarities with Velasquez were noted. So there was no sense in which Steer's painting could be found overly experimental by his friends, in displaying interest in Degas' style in the mid-1890s.

The long mirror was another device used most commonly in Degas' paintings of ballet rehearsals. Steer used it in several pictures of around 1894–5, most notably in two pictures of Rose, one seated, one standing. Both were exhibited at the NEAC in April 1895 and in both the model faces the mirror with her back to the viewer. The last picture was commented upon by R.A.M. Stevenson, who from this point emerged as a fairly consistent supporter of Steer. *The Looking Glass*, as *The Mirror, Model Seated* was originally known, he described as similar to Velasquez, no doubt referring to the handling of shadow surrounding the model. Beyond this he felt that Velasquez himself would have liked the work: "speaking for myself it possesses the fascinating power of forcing you to look out of the eyes of the painter. I hold it, therefore, to be genuine Impressionism" (BL 1971 62). Stevenson thereby confirms Steer's alliance with the historical traditions of Impressionism, as described in his own book on Velasquez. The initial conception carried through into a unified approach, the unity of vision that Steer himself had described to the Art Workers' Guild.

A third painting in this series *Girl Reading a Book*, from around 1895, is also of interest in terms of this rediscovery of more traditional sources. It is significant that it was possibly one of the last portraits of Rose Pettigrew. Their relationship ended, at her instigation by Rose's account. This is a loosely handled work, painted rapidly and with obvious brushmarks. The model's arm rests against the back of the chair, and she is absorbed in her book. The contrasts of tone, the lightness of her shawl with its dark fur edging and the darkness of the background suggest the influence both of Manet and Velasquez, as does the simple starkness of the composition and the relations of large areas of tone.

As noted earlier, Manet had always been preferred to Monet by the British critics. His more obvious concern for tradition, made him (like Degas) much more acceptable than Monet and Pissarro. So here also, Steer was sure of a safe response. And his preoccupation with Manet's influence continued for several years after 1895. After the break-up with Rose, Steer took on a succession of new models. Several of these were of a similar type to Manet's own models: dark-haired, sallow skinned and almond-eyed.

The best example, both of type of model chosen and theme depicted, is his *Nude Seated on a Bed* of 1896, an obvious reference to Manet's *Olympia*. But in comparison to Manet's own version Steer's picture admittedly appears rather weak and unconvincing. It is an experiment with style but one which seems to lack the individual quality that most of Steer's work retained. He gave it as a wedding present to MacColl.

A period of particularly intense interest in historical precedent and handling coincides with the departure of Rose after 1895. Specifically Steer became interested in reviving the manner of eighteenth century artists like Watteau and Fragonard, for a period of about five years. These pictures of extreme eclecticism seem superficially a bizarre episode in Steer's career. Looking back at them today, they have almost the qualities of kitsch; and they have frequently been dismissed as irrelevant capriciousness. What critics have failed to recognise though is that paintings like *The Toilet of Venus* and *The Pillow Fight* were exactly *about* style. The subject of the paintings –– the fleshy nudes — were as Laughton remarked, noticeably "less erotic than their prototypes" (BL 1971 70). They were primarily an extreme example of the exploration of style that informed his best landscapes in the years that followed, and so they constitute a period of great experimentation for Steer in this respect. The past became increasingly important for him, just as nostalgia and retrospection were a central part of the *content* of his Walberswick paintings. Here, in his evocation of past art, they became the *form* as well.

Studies like *The Rape of the Sabine Women* were not only in the style of the Old Master paintings, but were similar also in the methods used. MacColl records that Steer experimented with the glazing technique — the method whereby the subject is put down in monochrome and colour glazed over it (DSM 1945 107). It was quite a fashionable method at that time, used, for example, by Charles Shannon and Charles Furse. Steer's fascination with the grand manner of eighteenth century rococo art was shared by a number of artists and writers of the later 1890s. And yet the infatuation was not always successful with some critics even then. R.A.M. Stevenson's criticism of Tonks' painting in 1899 could equally have been applied by him to Steer's work in similar vein. Tonks, he wrote: "babbles in brush-work, stringing together scraps and phrases of style, ghostly reminiscences and fevered vision of Watteau, Gainsborough and Fragonard" (in DS 1965 30).

The later 1890s saw a series of exhibitions of British and French eighteenth century painting, and the market for such work was expanding rapidly: for example, Charles Wertheimer, Sargent's patron, was a keen collector and dealer. The appeal of the eighteenth century was simple escapism for most. W.E. Henley explained the allure of that period. "What attracts us", he wrote, "is its outside. We are in love with its houses and its china and its costumes. We are not enamoured with it as it was, but as it seems" (JHB 1945 168). It was the allure of another period that was the appeal for Steer. Roger Fry, in a later review of Steer, was reminded by the decorative aims of the *Toilet of Venus*, of that 1890s nostalgia for an "imaginary eighteenth century of conventional sensuality and sophisticated depravity" (DSM 1945 184).

There are of course connections between the appeal of the eighteenth century for painters like Steer, and the influence of rococo on the decorative movement of Art Nouveau, Charles Conder's designs, and the illustrations of Aubrey Beardsley. It is in this context that Steer's circle showed tendencies in common with the spirit of Art Nouveau, not in its decadence and overt posturing but in its general retreat from contemporary reality and conventional tastes. All shared a particular strain of snobbery in this sense, and as such the culture of the eighteenth century appealed to the instincts of the connoisseur.

The Goncourt brothers had popularised Fragonard's drawing in their *L'Art du XVIIIème Siecle*. It was an appeal which extended across the Channel, a love of artifice, superficial grace and elegance, an extension really of the aesthete's pursuit of beauty for its own sake. But in Steer's case the nostalgia was instinctive and genuine, not an affectation — a special perception of a vanished culture, prior to industrialisation and contemporary instability. It was discernible in its artistic legacy; even, for example, in Steer's collection of Chelsea figures and in the engravings of Fragonard, Watteau and Boucher which hung on the walls of his house in Cheyne Walk after 1898.

His painting of this period was a direct evocation of the style of the Old Masters. He imitated the slight, rhythmic brushstrokes of the nudes painted by Fragonard. In the light and texture and delicate atmosphere of *The Toilet of Venus*, he seems to have been attempting to recreate original sensibilities and actual perceptions. As C. Collins Baker wrote in 1909, his nudes recaptured what the highly polished nudes of Leighton had obscured: "the qualities in flesh and form that Tintoretto, Correggio and Watteau so wonderfully felt" (CCB 1909 263).

This was an exploration that went beyond mere pastiche, beyond the purely decorative and affected. It was a deliberate, painstaking attempt to recapture the inspiration and to recreate the atmosphere of what were described as the 'piquant gallantries' of a past age. Not a programme that would appeal to later modernists, but one that was well-rooted in a specific moment in culture at the end of the nineteenth century.

From the mid-1990s Steer began to be described more and more frequently as an 'instinctive' artist, and this has proved to be the most commonly applied definition of his skill ever since. William Rothenstein commented on an "instinctive rightness of judgement peculiar to a certain kind of Englishness" (WR 1932 171). In his review of Steer's Goupil exhibition, MacColl also commented on an "instinct for colour" and an "instinct for composition". For MacColl this lent an edge of risk and excitement to Steer's work. Unlike many contemporary painters who had "built a considerable amount of culture on a narrow base of instinct, Mr Steer works by instinct much more than by culture". As a result he could fail spectacularly at times, unlike the cultured painter for whom painting is "an affair of ropes and leading strings", who, by holding onto the ropes, "never comes a bad cropper, but also never gets anywhere". He is timid and always tasteful by comparison. Instinct can achieve much more than culture (DSM 1945 48-9).

Increasingly from the turn of the century, the term 'Englishness' was used to describe the special qualities of Steer's art and that of a growing number of contemporary artists. It is a problematic term, not least because some of the artists and writers concerned, while British, were not English. Ultimately the terms 'English' and 'British' became interchangeable, and served to suggest a cultural unity that could not in reality exist. 'Englishness' is therefore an extremely prejudicial term.

By the mid-1890s and throughout the 1900s a growing sense of nationalism, a concern to re-assert a spirit of Englishness, was evident in most areas of art and culture in this country. This clearly affected Steer, both in his work and in the general response to it. Earlier reactionary critics had warned young artists against travelling to France and being infected by foreign ideas, rather than concentrating on developing a solid national tradition in art. These were now echoed by some of the very artists who had once rejected such claims. Walter Sickert, looking back from 1910, gave credence to those early views:

> A painter is guided and pushed by his native surroundings very much as an actor is, and the atmosphere of English society, acting on a gifted group of painters, who had learnt what they knew either in Paris or from Paris has provided a school with aims and qualities altogether different from those of the Impressionists . . . . the Impressionists put themselves out more than we do in England. We all live like gentlemen, and keep gentlemen's hours (in OS 1947 57).

Perhaps there was some slight sarcasm in this last sentence. Nevertheless Sickert could almost have been thinking of Steer — his daily customs and rituals, his modesty and curious eccentricities.

Emma Steer had died in March 1898, aged 81. Steer and she had always been close, and her death was an obvious blow to him, increasing his isolation. As a result of his mother's death, however, Steer's financial circumstances were improved still further, with an inherited income now of £500 per year. He moved to Chelsea, to 109 Cheyne Walk, where he stayed for the rest of his life. He was accompanied in this move by Jane Raynes, who looked after him until her illness and subsequent death in 1929. She and Steer made a rather curious pair. Mrs Raynes was described as a 'devoted tyrant' and Steer, it seems, was able to develop his idiosyncrasies in comfort. The nurse affectionately regarded 'Mr Phibby' as still a small boy, and was certainly a protective mother figure for him. With her celebrated plain speaking and innate suspicion of cant and pretence she suffered no foolishness. She had a special dislike for George Moore. Steer's house became a central focus for the meetings of his by then established circle of friends. These were mostly male, and with Tonks, Brown, Gray and Moore in particular, mostly unmarried. It is from this point that the typical picture of Steer's circle emerges — long evening discussions on art-related subjects, led usually by Tonks, with Steer quietly dozing by the fireside. Behrend described Steer in these situations as "a perfect foil to Tonks's conversational brilliance". A similar description was given by Moore in his book *Conversations in Ebury Street*, although, characteristically, with the leading role in debate credited to himself. Steer commented drily on this aspect of the book when it was published in 1924. "You will note", he said in a letter to Behrend:

> that all the good things are said by Moore, and all the foolish things by Tonks or me — that's Moore all over, he may have literary integrity, but is bound by no scruples towards his friends.

Installed in Cheyne Walk with the security of his inherited income and his salary from the Slade, Steer was able to indulge his tastes and his passion for collecting. These tastes reflected that love of the eighteenth century. The house itself dated from around 1790, and Steer furnished it with Aubusson carpets, Regency and Louis XVI furniture, and increasingly cluttered it up with his hoardings — prints, china, coins, shells and minerals. Paintings included many by his friends, Ronald Gray, Tonks and Sargent for example. He also owned a collection of eighteenth century French engravings, admiring their greyness in comparison to more recent work. Giving in to his friends persuasions a studio was built to his specifications on the top floor, but it was rarely if ever used, Steer preferring to paint in a corner of the drawing room. As a result various objects and features of the room appeared in his figure paintings, contributing to the particular atmosphere of the works.

One specific example, typical of the development of his interior studies of the period, is *Hydrangeas*, dated 1901 and exhibited at the NEAC in the spring of that year. The model, Ethel Warwick, wears an antique lace shawl which had belonged to Steer's mother and is seated sideways on the large chintz sofa, teasing Steer's cat, Mr Thomas, with a pearl necklace. The flowers of the title fill in the bottom left hand corner of the canvas. The effect of this work today is highly sentimental and artificial, and would not have seemed out of place at a Royal Academy exhibition. MacColl, however, was full of praise for the handling of light and colour, for Steer's ability to make "living colour out of pigment". He stated that he "hardly dare expect to find anything in English painting so in tune with the *Ambarvalia*, its sacred light and flowers" (DSM 1945 53).

The central concern in the picture is the contrast of areas of pattern — the shawl, dress, sofa, and the atmosphere of these surface effects seen in sunlight. There is none of the intimation of character, the personal quality, seen in his portraits of Rose Pettigrew. The light atmospheric feel of this work characterises many of the domestic *genre* paintings of this period, both in Steer's own art and in that of several others. Tonks is an important figure in this context. His 'conversation pieces' produced in similar manner are often related to Steer's work of this kind, and his dominating personality may have had much to do with their emergence. Walter Russell, a Slade colleague, is another example — producing domestic interiors and figure compositions with a restrained form of Impressionism which in some hands, Russell's included, is often overly refined, aiming too much at the creation of period atmosphere. The word 'atmosphere' was in fact used widely in contemporary writing associated with these pictures, describing the concern with air and light. Frank Rutter commented on its use:

> Atmosphere was the magic word of the time . . . . Either a work of art had atmosphere — and it was allright; or it did not — and it was all wrong (FR 1933 65).

With Steer, Tonks, Russell and Brown at their head, the Slade and the NEAC were dominated by what can be viewed as a 'new romantic' tendency. Visible in this was that same nostalgic retrospection, a desire to conserve a spirit of the past, that also dominates Steer's art. As Rutter went on, artists in this period "felt that something was slipping away . . . a settled and rather beautiful way of life which has now gone never to return" (ibid 66). This spirit is also witnessed in Steer's taste for antiques, the faded interiors and the understated delicacy of his domestic scenes — which is ultimately their primary aim.

Those qualities that characterise *Hydrangeas* reappear to an extent in *The Music Room*, and perhaps finally in *The End of the Chapter* in 1911. *The Music Room* was exhibited at the NEAC in 1906. This highly composed portrayal of two women musicians is in fact a new version of the theme of that very early painting, *Andante*. As in *Hydrangeas* the figures in *The Music Room* wear dresses that date from the mid-nineteenth century, a deliberate attempt to evoke the atmosphere of that earlier age. The reviewer in *The Studio* was much impressed by Steer's delicate handling of shadow and his subtlety of observation. Only in the actual brushwork, which is thickly applied using a palette knife in places, did the writer find an interruption to the mood of the work — "the elegance of his scheme, its classic dignity of restfulness and perfection" (*The Studio* 1906 225).

The romantic nostalgia of pictures like this one, and the elegant atmospheric interiors of Tonks, were rejected by the more radical young artists from the Slade. But around the turn of the century they did have some influence on the work of various students and ex-students. Orpen is one noted example, and he had particular respect for Steer.

A fascination with the technical grace of eighteenth century artists like Watteau was also passed on to the students in the late 1890s. C.H. Collins Baker's appendix to Hone's biography of Tonks described how John and Orpen assimilated into their draughtsmanship the "form-expressive line" of the eighteenth century artist, and also the "living beauty of pose, gesture and drapery" — aspects which Tonks and Steer strove to reflect in their own art at this time. Tonks always had enormous respect for Augustus John in particular; although he may have disapproved of his personality he found him the greatest draughtsman the Slade had ever produced.

The complimentary reviews which pictures like *Hydrangeas* received represent such a marked contrast to those of the early to mid nineties, that one again feels Steer may have deliberately set out to paint pictures that would go down well with critics and friends — for the sake of peace and quiet as much as anything else. As mentioned earlier, several writers have commented on Tonks' bearing in this respect. He had an early enthusiasm for the Pre-Raphaelites, and therefore for a high degree of finish. This made him unsympathetic to some of Steer's more loosely handled works. His nagging of Steer on that subject, his declaration that "we must finish", had its effect, finally, in pictures of Steer's such as *The Muslin Dress* and *The End of the Chapter*. The latter, painted in 1911, effectively signals the end of this phase of *genre* scenes. Presumably then with Tonks' complaints in mind, the handling of *The Music Room*, with its dazzling and dissolving effects of sunlight, is replaced by a polished naturalism and a meticulous observation of detail. For MacColl, *The End of the Chapter* was painted "somewhat in the spirit of a wager" and is marked "by that impurity of origin" (DSM 1945 108). He preferred works where Steer had expressed his own instinctive selection of detail and his innate sense of unity of vision.

Like *The Music Room, The End of the Chapter* was painted in his own drawing room in Cheyne Walk. The extreme naturalistic detail of the picture produces a work which for Steer is regressive in style, but at least gives sound documentary evidence of his tastes in furnishings, china and so on. The model, Lilian Montgomery, wears a dress belonging to the 1860s, again owned by Steer. Having supposedly laid down her book she is warming her hands by the fireside. The obvious artificiality of the scene adds to the rather lifeless character of the painting. Like *Hydrangeas*, this figure study shows none of the sense of character and personality that we find in the portraits of Rose Pettigrew. As Roger Fry later remarked, *The End of the Chapter* is a *"nature morte,* deliberately arranged" (Fry 1911 396). Lacking in atmosphere and expressive handling of paint, Fry hoped that *The End of the Chapter* would also mark the end of an unsuccessful episode in Steer's art.

From just after the turn of the century Steer was becoming increasingly known as a landscapist rather than a figure or portrait painter, and he himself seems to have been much happier with this view, turning down commissions for portraits on fairly thin grounds. To Lady Howard de Walden, he remarked later that he was not a portrait painter, but that he could "do a small landscape of her". Steer was not especially good at expressing personality in paint unless he had some specific relationship with the sitter, and his comment was no doubt meant to imply this.

But although Steer's portraits give little psychological insight into the character of his sitters, they did create a perfect model for further stylistic experimentation, and the evocation of mood and atmosphere. A good example of this is the portrait of *Mrs Violet Hammersley* of 1906, painted in the same year as *The Music Room.*

Hugh Hammersley and his family were friends of Steer from the early days at Cheyne Walk, and their house in Hampstead was one of the few that he would bother to visit outside Chelsea. Hammersley was a banker and collector, and alongside paintings by Steer he owned works by Sickert, Tonks, Sargent and William Rothenstein. He and his wife entertained these artists along with MacColl, Augustus John and Max Beerbohm on Sunday afternoons. Violet Hammersley, Hugh's sister-in-law, remembered these occasions and her first meeting with Steer in 1902. She was struck by the static figure, rarely moving from his seat, keeping fairly quiet but always appreciative of a good joke, often adding the odd witty remark. He enjoyed the gossip but without any trace of malice. For the portrait Violet Hammersley wore a dress by Worth, again from an earlier period, lent to her by Mrs Hugh Hammersley. She recalls the sitting lasting through into the summer of the following year. This was at Cheyne Walk, in the drawing room by the French windows. Conversation was lively, it seems, much of it about finances, Violet's family business, and was always a source of interest to Steer.

The portrait which resulted is notable particularly for its obvious reference to the painterly style of the eighteenth century — Boucher's *Madame Pompadour* is one such source. It also refers to Gainsborough, with its light, feathery brushstrokes, soft colouring, and the landscape setting which conforms to the conventions of the eighteenth century — dense foliage on the right of the canvas, rolling away, following the folds of the oyster coloured dress to the pastoral countryside on the left. It is, in effect, an elegant pastiche of 'the grand style', an aesthetic fantasy that sought to establish some kind of natural relationship between the sitter and the rustic landscape surrounding her.

Steer was an enthusiastic admirer of Gainsborough, and MacColl felt the two had qualities and tastes in common. Both preferred to paint landscapes rather than portraits, neither were bookish, and both had an intuitive grasp of compositional style with no time for academicism in art. The reticence and detachment of Gainsborough in his portraits, is perhaps another characteristic that he and Steer shared. Gainsborough's popularity was at a height generally in those years, and the price of his works was increasing rapidly as interest mounted, not only here but in Europe and America too. Charles Wertheimer was a notable collector of Gainsborough, and Orpen's 1908 portrait of him showed in the background his Gainsborough portrait of Miss Linley.

Writers of the period sought to establish links between Gainsborough and the French Impressionists. In 1905 Frederick Wedmore made connections with Renoir in the "miracle of finesse" (KF 1984 212) that saved the French artist's work from the dangers of triviality. For MacColl Gainsborough along with Wilson were the "great names" in landscape. They "made English" the art of Claude and Rubens. He credited to them the English painter's preoccupation with natural light and atmosphere — an influence, as he said, which could be "traced beyond the bounds of pure landscape" (DSM 1945 146). It was an instinctive, immediate response to the natural world.

MacColl and Steer valued Gainsborough's poetic sensibility. To them he was a poet-painter, and the poetic vision was expressed in the way he applied paint to canvas — in his actual brushstrokes. This was the essence of Steer's approach, the effort to express feelings through technique.

As Clive Bell later described, Gainsborough's brushwork was like handwriting — "the immediate expression of what the artist felt for what he saw" (RSL 1938 33-4). And MacColl would have been happy to make similar claims for Steer — it was the search for 'congruous beauty' that attracted his friend to Gainsborough. Bell described Gainsborough as a "singing painter". He needed to feel some instinctive empathy with his subject in order to express it well. If this empathy was not present then the subject could at times appear stiff and lifeless. A criticism that applies also to Steer and explains the lifeless quality of some of his figure studies, his reluctance to paint commissioned portraits, and the exceptional quality of many of his landscape paintings.

Nature and Nostalgia

The beginning of a fundamental change in Steer's painting of landscapes first became noticeable in one particular picture of 1893, *A Classic Landscape*, which had been included in the exhibition at Goupils. This was a painting of Richmond Bridge in very thin muted tones, reminiscent of the extreme atmospheric effects of some of Monet's pictures of Argenteuil from the 1870s. But beyond this there is, in the setting and in the breadth of the work, a clear sign of a shift in interest to much earlier sources — indications of Claude and of landscape painting from the beginning of the nineteenth century, of Turner. In this Steer was returning to the very sources of Impressionism, as repeatedly stressed in the slightly later writings of Frederick Wedmore, Wynford Dewhurst and MacColl, and which confirmed a reassertion of the importance of tradition. Those writers had consistently recounted Monet and Pissarro's visit to London in 1870 and the deep impact of their encounter with Turner — the influence of the lights and shadows in his handling of colour, his sunrises and sunsets, the dissolving web of light and its reflections on surfaces of his late work, especially with its apparent lack of drawing. Turner was the first Impressionist, in their view. In the first instance this reference back to Turner served in the effort to make French Impressionism more palatable to British audiences. A fairly straightforward appeal to nationalistic sensibilities developed from these repeated emphases, and little attention was paid to the fact that the French painters, Pissarro in particular, disputed any substantial influence.

A Classic Landscape was accompanied by two other paintings — *The Thames From Richmond Hill*, a small sketch or panel, and *Syon House*, a view from across the Thames. All three bear witness to the wide sweeping vistas of Turner's landscapes. It was an open format which became characteristic of Steer's later landscapes, preferring wide expanses of scenery to small crowded corners and even disliking trees to the extent that they "got in the way".

Steer had been introduced to Turner's art from an extremely early age, encouraged by his father, who taught the young boy that Turner was "the greatest painter". When he was a child a Turner watercolour hung in his bedroom where the light fell, and he told MacColl that "he never came to an end of it" (DSM 1945 14). For the years following 1895, a good many of Steer's summer painting trips were essentially tours of Turner's sites — efforts to find the exact spot. MacColl remembered him carrying a copy of Turner's *Liber Studiorum* in his pocket on these pilgrimages to Yorkshire and the Welsh Borders. And yet while at times Steer's scenes are Turnerian, the technique can often vary and show stylistic influences from other artists. As Andrew Forge put it, after 1895 he began to study the "classical machinery of landscape composition" (AF 1960 7), and the range of sources used varied widely over the next five years to include Gainsborough, Constable, Corot and Monticelli.

Steer began his summer visits in search of the quintessential English landscape — the traditional landscape of Turner and later of Constable — with a visit to Richmond, Yorkshire in 1895, accompanied by Brown and W.C. Coles, Master of Winchester School of Art.

The end of the nineteenth century and the turn of the twentieth witnessed a widespread cultural re-evaluation of the English countryside. In large measure this phenomenon relates to that spirit of nationalism and insecurity referred to already, and was therefore very different to the rustic naturalists' interest in the daily activities of the peasantry. Steer's later landscapes largely ignore the figure, other than as an occasional note within the composition. Landscape artists from the later 1890s were at the beginning of a movement of artists who sought, however unconsciously, to re-establish a national identity in their re-presentation of their own country. It was a programme of innate patriotism, and the critical language with which it was described increased in fervour at a time of national unease, of mounting social and political instability. The experience of imperial decline and paranoia over Britain's international standing up to the First World War, alongside labour struggles and agricultural depression, all contributed to a climate of increasing introspection, in which European Modernism was out of place.

Aspects of social class are clearly an important issue in this context. The reshaping of traditional class boundaries, which was the legacy of the Industrial Revolution, had by the close of the nineteenth century amounted to conflict and a sense of unease within the established middle classes. In effect, Steer, Brown and MacColl and their circle belonged to this older section by dint of the family background and upbringing that they mostly shared. The attacks on the philistines in matters of art had entailed a fair degree of snobbery and a distaste for the aspirations and standards of the uncivilised usurpers — the "brewers or distillers" as they chose to characterise them. However sardonically put, all of this points to a general lack of security over their own social position as the 'genuine' middle class. In the face of possible displacement, the exploration of the English countryside was an effort to assert the values of the past and of their traditional heritage. This was not a new phenomenon, it had recurred regularly since the early years of the Industrial Revolution. But it is of interest especially in the context of painters who had been Francophiles, who at an earlier stage professed progressive ideologies for their art. Yet in a fairly short time they were seeking out the special qualities of their own national culture, and displaying a nostalgia for a perceived view of rural England.

This ruralism reverberates consistently throughout the end of the nineteenth century and the beginning of the twentieth. A growing antipathy towards business and a reassertion of the values of gentlemanly existence coincides with the fascination for that idealised view of eighteenth century culture in which the constructed image of the rural gentry reached its peak. This evoked the benign patronage of the country squire for his cottagers and the organic, natural relationship that was assumed to exist between them. A hearty dislike for urban life and the grime of the city, from which Steer made his annual escape, was implied in much of the art of the period. The notable exception to this trend was Walter Sickert, who, on his return to London from Dieppe in 1905, continued his exploration of urban themes in his dispassionate representations of shopkeepers and innkeepers, music halls and the seamier sides of everyday life in Camden Town. It was a deliberate

decision to portray the mundane existence of ordinary people —
one that Steer found increasingly difficult to comprehend. Why, he
asked, did Sickert persist in treating these "ugly-beautiful
subjects?" Steer's own aesthetic was much more in accord with
general cultural inclinations. His anti-urban sensibility was echoed
time and again in writings right up to the First World War and
afterwards. This was expressed most clearly in 1909 in a
description of London, which, it was written, "now stinks and
reverberates; to live in it is to live in the hollow of a clanging bell, to
breathe its air is to breathe the foulness of modern progress" (IJ
1983 28). A far cry from Sickert's appeal to artists to express the
"magic and poetry of London's streets".

Steer's perception of the English landscape embodied the spirit
of nostalgia and retrospection that, in different ways, had been
central to much of his painting up to this point. It can be detected in
the far-away gazes of the young women on Walberswick Pier, the
unselfconscious innocence of the children playing on the beaches,
even the reflective attitude of some of his portraits of Rose
Pettigrew, and also in the atmospheric re-creations of a past life in
the 'fancy pictures' in the style of Watteau, Fragonard et al. There
is an allusive quality about all of this, a sense of association,
implications of some 'otherness' which is peculiar to Steer's
painting throughout his lifetime, born out of private
considerations, elements of his own character, but which also relate
to art more generally throughout the 1900s.

In the type of landscape that Steer was drawn to, he was also
reflecting a national preoccupation. He painted the scenery which
increasing numbers of people were beginning to visit on their
annual holidays, and painted it with a sensitivity that appealed to a
wider public than he had previously managed to attract. That first
trip to Richmond in 1895 was, as previously mentioned, inspired
by the tours of Turner, but it also appealed to Steer's own sense of
the picturesque. As MacColl put it, Steer showed from the
beginning a "deep, exclusive love for England for the 'old bones of
his country' " (DSM 1945 76), and he found his ideal sites in the
castles and rivers that Turner had valued. A fondness for the
picturesque was common among landscape artists at the end of the
century — the atmosphere, the sense of time past as visible in the
decaying structures of *Richmond Castle* and *Easby Abbey* appealed

to Steer on the level of romantic nostalgia that informed his work in general. In this Steer and his peers were involved in a process of aestheticising the countryside, linking art and nature. The depiction of dilapidated scenery implied a sense of loss, the loss of an old order, a distant way of life. There seems to be some confusion here between, on the one hand a topographical tour, and on the other a conscious search for the picturesque.

In his depiction of nature, in this respect, Steer is concerned with the association of time and place. And the search for the 'right' site, or the 'August' site, as Sickert jokingly put it, was crucial. In these earlier landscapes of Steer's the Impressionist technique of loose but systematically applied brushstrokes and brighter colour is put to work on scenes that were largely painted out of doors. In these and in the landscapes that follow, Steer continued his by now well-established method of adopting style and technique according to the particular view and his chosen expression of it. The Impressionist method related directly to painting nature out of doors on sunny days. It was used by growing numbers of artists in these years, most of whom were associated with the NEAC, including Lavery, Sargent, and less well known painters like Wynford Dewhurst.

The following year, 1896, the three travelled to Barnard Castle in County Durham, and Steer produced two views of the castle, one seen from the river. Again this was following in the footsteps of Turner. The pattern of summer visits and landscape painting was now set, while the autumn and winter months were spent on portraits or figure compositions in the studio. 1896 was the year he produced *The Rape of the Sabines, The Pillow Fight* and *Girl on the Bed*, pictures which highlight the extreme eclecticism and historicism of his enterprise and his display of retrospective nostalgia through styles of painting which best expressed the type of subject.

In the summer of 1897 he travelled once more to Yorkshire, to Knaresborough, again with Brown and Coles. The works which resulted once again reflected his preoccupation with picturesque scenery. *The Vista*, a tree-framed path leading through to the old viaduct, was one of a series of paintings of an avenue of oak trees. The numerous sketches are evidence of his deliberate search for the 'right' spot. Steer employed Impressionist method in terms of colour and handling, but the scene is orchestrated in a very deliberate and composed manner. He is not content simply to record the transitory effects of nature according to the ethics of French Impressionism. His concern to impose design and structure onto the scene and to select compositional elements is typical of British versions of Impressionism, but also equate here with the picturesque tendency, that urge to aestheticise the countryside in the manner of artists and theorists from the late eighteenth and early nineteenth centuries.

In *An Oak Avenue* bright sunlight reflects through the dense foliage of the trees surrounding the path. It is a womb-like enclosed view, a sheltered idyll. In strict stylistic terms the sources for this picture would include work by Gainsborough, Constable and Corot, and in the technique Impressionist painters like Pissarro were also influential. Many sources are used in one painting, but the overall feel of the picture is Steer's own. It is tempting to interpret this kind of image as almost reflective of Steer's own state of mind at the time, the melancholic tendency and the isolation that he appears to have experienced during these years despite the constant companionship of artists such as Brown and Tonks. In this respect the picture functions almost as sanctuary for the artist in a personal sense. A painting like *An Oak Avenue* can perhaps therefore be read almost as an equivalent to Steer's own lack of personal and emotional security.

Martin Wiener has commented on the generally increased importance of rural and ancient places, as a counterbalance to the disillusionment with the city and ideas of progress at this point at the close of the nineteenth century. The search for the past was a fairly common phenomenon, as we have seen. It was a sensibility that encompassed both radical and reactionary ideologies. In the literary field the ruralist tendency was best exemplified by the then Poet Laureate, Alfred Austin, who published his *Haunts of Ancient Peace* in 1901 — the title taken from Tennyson's *English Idylls*. Austin had travelled throughout the country in search of "Old England, or so much of it is left" and concluded that he had found "ancientness in abundance". The idealisation of the English countryside increased during these years hand in hand with the anti-urban response. As Wiener remarked, this resulted in an atmosphere in which the countryside functioned as, in his terms, a "psychic balance and a refuge" (MW 1985 47). In contemporary literature Austin's tone was shared by writers like Edward Thomas, Thomas Hardy and Richard Jefferies. In painting, Steer's vision of a rural Arcadia would also be expressed, but in a rather more grandiose manner, by landscape artists such as Arnesby Brown, Alfred East and David Murray, who developed a stylistic synthesis of Turner, Constable and Impressionism into large and commercially successful paintings, exhibited at the Academy. Arnesby Brown in particular was known for producing picture after picture of contented cattle, the 'lowing herd', grazing in idyllic settings. But as one writer has put it: "where Murray was composing careful pastiche, Steer was concerned with meta-morphosis" (KM 1989 141). His method and style related specifically to his own perceptions and desired expression of the subject.

As the nineteenth century closed, the gradual decline of the Empire contributed to a sentimental view of the countryside, and ensured a continued popularity for images like those of Arnesby Brown's. In literature this paradigm spread into the verse of Georgian poets such as Edward Marsh and Rupert Brooke, and in novels it emerged in works prior to the First World War such as E.M. Forster's *Howard's End*. It became a constant feature of English cultural life. A hackneyed stereotype in some cases, or a refusal to accept reality as the idealisation developed obsessive proportions.

Steer's own constant stylistic experimentation meant that his vision was saved from clichéd repetition, even if the thematic tenor of his work varied relatively little. From the late nineties he became increasingly interested in the paintings of Monticelli, then popular in his circle. Steer in fact owned some of his works, admiring, as MacColl described, his "powdering of light upon trees" (DSM 1945 127). The crude intensity of his colours and the thick impasted brushstrokes allowed an element of expressive freedom. And his influence on Steer is evident in *The Embarkment*, a painting completed in 1901. Laughton describes how Steer developed from Monticelli the idea of thick paint as an "equivalent for visual sensation" (BL 1971 87). The search for equivalents, a consistent feature of Steer's work, achieves even greater physical emphasis in this respect. In *The Embarkment*, Monticelli's heavy pigment is employed in the dense background of trees, in front of which Steer returns to one of his earlier themes of young women by the water's edge, here stepping aboard the punt. An idyllic scene of rural peace and tranquillity has re-emerged and been given new expressive possibilities through changing styles of representation.

But the search for British precedents to Impressionism, witnessed by Steer's enthusiasm for Turner, emerged also at the end of the century with his growing interest in Constable as a source of inspiration. And in this he found critical support from MacColl, and from a wider public as well. The developing admiration for Constable is one further symptom of the ruralist nostalgia of the period in general, and of the taste for the picturesque. Constable's own retreat from urban reality into the rural idylls of his own native surroundings at the beginning of the nineteenth century had clear connections with the situation at the end of that century. The way in which he invested his scenery with associated personal meanings is, of course, another parallel with Steer's own tendencies.

The growing interest in Constable among artists and collectors was witnessed by a large exhibition of his work held at the Cornhill Gallery in 1899, but by this time the market for his work was already well-established, with Charles Holmes emerging as the acknowledged expert and writer on Constable by 1900. Like Steer with Turner, Holmes had spent the middle part of the 1890s looking for Constable's sites in the Stour Valley. In 1902 he published his *Constable and his Influence on Landscape Painting*, in which he was mostly interested in the early work — for the "alternation between tradition and nature" (CH 1902 115) — an aspect that would also interest Steer in particular.

Holmes' book was the most authoritative of a number of works on Constable published around this time, an indication of the widespread popularity of the artist. More obvious signs are visible in the fact that Thomas Cook & Sons were advertising 'A Visit to Constable Country' in 1893 and more and more of his work was finding its way into public collections, and was sold to rich American buyers. For popular opinion, Constable's paintings represented that old rural order that was felt to be in danger of disappearing. Percy Lindley's 'A Drive Through Constable Country' sums up the appeal:

> So closes a pleasant day in this cheerful Constable country, a
> country of cornfields and sloping river banks; . . . of spacious
> valleys and sparkling distances of woods with gray church towers;
> and sunlight and shadow playing over all (IFW & LP 1984 112).

For the serious critics, and for Steer too, Constable's value lay in
the way in which he stepped beyond mere naturalism, aware of its
limitations, towards a style that displayed an increasing sense of
pictorial unity by which he could depict the shifting movements of
nature with a greater breadth of vision. In this respect Constable,
like Turner, could be described as another precursor to, or, as
Kenneth Clark later described him, a "prophet of Impressionism".
And in this way Impressionism itself was further established as a
logical outcome of tradition, and of British tradition to boot. This
was exactly the tone of Wynford Dewhurst's *Impressionist Painting*,
which was put together from a series of articles written by him in
journals such as *The Studio* during the later 1890s. Doubtless
thinking of Steer, Dewhurst wrote:

> Englishmen who are taunted with following the methods of the
> French Impressionists, sneered at for imitating a foreign style, are
> in reality but practising their own, for the French artists simply
> developed a style which was British in its conception (WD 1904 3–
> 6).

Constable and Turner, it was noted, worked out in the open like
the French painters. They could therefore record more reliably the
transitory effects of nature, and of light in particular. Dewhurst also
found similarities in technique, in the side by side dabs of pure
colour. The only significant difference, according to this writer, was
the influence of the art of Japan on the French painters and their
curious handling of perspective, plus a greater brightness of colour
in the Impressionists' palette.

In their constant search to forge parallels between artists on
either side of the Channel some writers, as here, often overstated
Constable's 'Impressionist' method, and blatantly ignored the very
idealised and subjective view of the English countryside that the
artist presented. It was for this constructed evocation of rustic
landscape that he was most prized by the public. Important also
was the strongly autobiographical feel of his work — that sense of
the painter's natural environment. This was important to Steer as

well, as MacColl had noted. In this respect Constable's example was crucial to the particular attitude towards English art that developed throughout the 1890s and on into the next century. Even Kenneth Clark in the passage cited earlier expressed this view. From Constable, Clark found the:

> guarantee that England is supremely paintable. Probably the only country that English artists should paint. The whole aesthetic of landscape painting must involve a profound intimacy with the countryside portrayed (RSL 1938 41).

It was as a painter in this category, and as a descendant of Constable, that Steer was increasingly viewed.

In 1898 Steer visited Ludlow in Shropshire, which was in effect a return to the countryside of his youth along the Welsh Borders. As Frank Rutter later suggested, his childhood exploration with his father of the "rolling, fertile prospects" of the Wye Valley may have implanted "that love of lucent expanses of pastoral and wooded country" (RI 1943 6). And the instinctive nationalism that is often cited as part of Steer's character emerged in his landscape paintings from this date onwards with increased emphasis.

On this first trip to Ludlow he painted *Bird-Nesting* from the banks of the River Teme, a site he returned to later in 1906 and studied from various angles and positions. Steer's habit of scrutinising his site from different points was caricatured by Max Beerbohm in an illustration subtitled: 'The landscape becomes fidgety as Wilson Steer goes for a walk'. The carefully selected view here is taken from the top of the bank, looking sharply down towards children playing below, with trees on either side of the canvas, with the dark broody skies above that he began to admire most. The paint is dark, with vivid notes, and is dense and thickly applied. In style it suggests influence from both Constable and Pissarro, but the sheer physicality of the paint itself also refers to Monticelli's handling. In other similar works, often repainted later, frequently using a palette knife, the thickness reached such proportions that Steer would joke that he could tell by its weight if a picture was really finished (DSM 1945 109).

The thickness of pigment undeniably asserts the importance of the medium in Steer's painting. C. Collins Baker noted in Steer a "rare appreciation of the varying properties of oil paint, its transparence and liquid impasto" (CCB 1909 259-66). This aspect of Steer's work has the effect of drawing attention to the processes of representation, of seeing and transcribing. In so doing he avoids producing straightforward pastiches of Constable's style, which lesser artists of the period were wont to do. With Steer, here as always, the style and technique create the meaning, his expression of the landscape.

Ludlow Castle, Stormy Sky, produced from the same visit, is an example of Steer's special fondness for wide open landscapes and big stormy skies which feature prominently in his work from this point. This is a wide vista painted from on high, with the bridge in the low foreground and the castle in the middle distance to the extreme right of the canvas. The steep wooded bank descending from the left towards the river draws the eye in to the picturesque collection of buildings below. Frank Rutter has also claimed that it was from his early knowledge of this countryside that Steer was able to "grasp the pictorial possibilities of broad distant prospects" (RI 1943 6) in his mature work, and, as with Constable, the possibilities for studying light and weather which these prospects allowed. Steer's friend Sargent had commented that in Constable one often found a thunderstorm and a fine day going on at the same time — which can almost be said of some of Steer's own canvases from these years.

The predilection for changeable skies that he associated with the English landscape involved no small measure of discomfort for Steer, who was as a result open to all the vagaries of weather — a potential misery for him, with his habitual fear of draughts and sudden chills. In later years this fear led to the recounted tales of him donning a hat to go from one room in his house to another in case the temperature should drop on the staircase. As years progressed, he appears to have steadily increased the amounts of clothing required on his painting expeditions to quite bizarre proportions, with high collars, not unlike a parson's, and layer upon layer of waistcoats, jackets and coats. These could all be assembled in various ways depending on the variations of heat and cold. Yet in his determination to find the perfect site, he was apparently willing to accept the lack of comfort. His constant fussiness, however tongue in cheek, provided amusement for his companions. Philip Connard, who often joined the annual excursions in later years, is quoted as saying that Steer's requirements were, in order of importance: "1. shelter from the wind, 2. proximity to a lavatory, 3. shade from the sun, 4. protection from children, and 5. subject" (DSM 1945 119).

Steer's innate stoicism was necessary to endure the constant aggravations involved in his outdoor painting and sketching activities — the sun's disappearance when painting a sunny scene, and its reappearance on painting a grey landscape. Rain fàlling on sketches, the irritation of flies and inquisitive farmers and tourists — all had to be borne with resignation. Friends commented that on occasions his preoccupation with comfort did overcome his willingness to accept these hardships, and from time to time, according to notes written by G.L. Behrend, Steer's friend and a later painting companion, a subject might be chosen for its comfortable viewpoint rather than for its own intrinsic merit. Behrend also believed that Steer's physical lethargy was pertinent here, and possibly hindered his potentialities as a painter. He claimed that this was a likely reason for his frequent disinclination to finish off a picture — either the work 'came off', or it didn't and was never completed. Years later it was even suggested that it was this very lethargy that prevented Steer from continuing his Impressionist studies, and as a result, paintings produced in studio were in part an avoidance of having to work out of doors. In contrast to the notion of Steer abandoning pictures out of laziness, however, was the fact that he tended at times to overwork a canvas, and this overpainting sometimes destroyed the original freshness of conception. A particular example of this is cited in Behrend's notes. A large oil of Chepstow Castle was virtually sold to a Japanese collector. Steer, however, decided to "do a little more to it", and so far altered the effect of the work that the buyer withdrew, and the picture was apparently 'knocked down' at forty guineas at the Christie's sale in 1942. MacColl himself admits that one work re-emerged from the studio as "a monster of rehandling", although he adds that, at times, his paintings benefited superbly from this process (DSM 1945 109).

Both the overpainting and the habitual abandonment of paintings that weren't 'right', point to the fact that the overall design, the composition of the pictorial image and the arrangement of all the elements of the work, were crucial to Steer. In this he went far beyond any attempt merely to record the scene. This, of course, is the essence of landscape painting in the picturesque tradition, and was noted by reviewers such as C.Collins Baker, who read in pictures like *The Vista* and *Bird-Nesting* Steer's deliberate pursuit of stately decoration and simplification. In the majority of cases, this was the tone of opinion on Steer's art around 1900, except in circumstances where the density of the pigment was considered too extreme by the reviewer. This in fact was the response of a writer who described *The Embarkment* as an "outrage", an "uneasy labouring after an easy technique" (in JM 1985 46), indicating that the old taste for smooth surfaces and high finish still prevailed in some quarters.

Increasingly though, Steer was regarded positively, both by friends and a growing public as *the* successor to Constable. His vision, like that of Constable, was said to express those special qualities, the 'atmosphere', of the British countryside, with a lyricism and instinct that was natural to this country's traditions. Some, MacColl included, were to go so far as to suggest that Steer was a better painter than Constable. Collins Baker felt he had "more knowledge of skies". Frank Rutter believed he had made the broad expanses of the particular kind of landscape so much his own that, he remarked, "when we see it on our journeying, we say — Look! that's a regular Steer" — an observation he felt could be made of no other English landscape painter since Constable (FR 1933 28).

In this context, such a concept of cultural unity invoked through the term 'Englishness' was further elaborated to apply to the two artists. A passage written in the 1930s by Eric Newton illustrates this:

> The word English as applied to art means a great deal. It means the opposite of fanatic, it means the opposite of intellectualised, it frequently means technically competent, it usually means romantic. Mr Steer's landscapes . . . . have all those qualities (RSL 1938 57).

In Newton's terms those qualities of Englishness are wholly positive attributes compared to the extremely negative sense in which he perceives Modernism, and this is one further example of attempts by writers to divorce Steer from European influence.

In June 1902 Steer held his second one-man exhibition, this time at the Carfax Gallery. Over half the works exhibited there were watercolours, including the watercolour version of *The Embarkment*. Watercolours represented an increasing proportion of Steer's output from this point on, appearing in the first instance as preparatory studies produced out of doors. MacColl mentions the current vogue for wash-drawings rather than the more worked-up watercolour paintings exhibited at the Royal Societies. Hercules Brabazon had also significantly influenced Steer's generation with his gouache drawings, his works having been exhibited by Steer's dealer David Croal Thompson and widely appreciated. Steer's own substantial use of watercolour began around the time of his trip to Knaresborough in 1900. Prior to this time he had viewed the practice in a fairly negative light — describing it as 'whoring' and later commenting that "Watercolour is like a cow eating grass, oil painting like a cow chewing the cud". For the most part watercolours were a means for exploring a subject in preparation for treatment in oil. In watercolour he could work with a greater degree of freedom. His habitual comments that a work either 'came off' or it didn't applied particularly in this case, and those which did 'come off' he counted simply as flukes.

As years progressed, however, his skill at and taste for this medium increased considerably, and it has quite often been viewed as one of the most successful aspects of his work as a whole. But it was an area in which he felt instinct played the largest role. He remarked that he would find it impossible to give a lesson in watercolour painting. His natural abilities at the elimination of unnecessary detail, at achieving colour harmony and total atmospheric effect combined most successfully here, and these were difficult skills to pass on in his teaching. Steer's admiration for English eighteenth and early nineteenth century artists would also give him a taste for watercolour, with Girtin and Cotman as examples.

The majority of the works done in the early period from 1900 to around 1905 were produced on the summer painting expeditions along the Welsh Borders, to Stroud, Bridgnorth and Ludlow, and were conceived very much in the spirit of exploratory and preliminary sketches for the oil paintings of these sites. And yet, as Cal Clothier notes, he quickly became aware of the value and intrinsic qualities of the medium itself. His concern with finding the right technique to express the subject was realised perfectly in this sense. Water was a prominent feature in many of his landscapes. Clothier points out that Steer was, to a large extent, using water to depict water. The paper, as another material, could be used to express light (CC 1985 23-31). So watercolour was for him an ideal medium in which to explore the effects of light and form with much greater ease and spontaneity than oils allowed.

As mentioned, between 1900 and the period just prior to the First World War Steer was to be viewed primarily as a landscape painter, and by a growing number of writers as the true successor to Turner and Constable, and the best living example of the continuing tradition of 'Englishness' in art. It was a reputation which he bore with characteristic modesty, and no doubt some amusement given the earlier treatment and criticism he had received. During this period he painted most frequently in sites along the borders of Wales. Hereafter his excursions were mainly limited to the southern end of the country — partly through predilection and partly obvious practicality. In this however he was typical of that generation of artists, writers and the 'cultured' middle classes who found 'Englishness' in the South. Northern areas signified industry and grime, despite the vast areas of open countryside — without doubt class bias is pertinent here. As noted, the countryside on the edges of Wales held rich associative meanings for Steer, much of it explored with his father. The terrain in this area was, as we have seen, his preferred type — gently rolling with wide vistas and large open skies. The castles and monuments, many of them previously painted by Turner, perfectly reflected Steer's taste for the picturesque in their various states of decay.

Much of the original elaboration of picturesque theory had resulted from the Reverend Gilpin's travels around the Wye Valley in the late eighteenth century. In his observations of that area in 1783, Gilpin had urged the painter to depict it roughness and irregularity, to look for character and not perfection — this opinion had directly influenced Turner and Girtin in their tours of the area and in their choice of particular sites, the most popular being Tintern Abbey and Chepstow Castle.

Steer's own visits some hundred years later were made usually in the company of Brown and Coles, who continued together on these annual painting trips for around twenty one years, according to Brown's sister. The trips constituted for Steer the "acme of discomfort", so persistent was his wish to explore the exact same sites previously visited by Turner. But considering Turner's famous lack of concern for physical hardship and difficult conditions, he and Steer could not have been less alike. Steer's contemporaries often remembered the contrast between his periods in London and his teaching, as compared to his summer painting trips — the passivity, even laziness of the former, and the determined activity of the latter — a counter to Behrend's opinion.

In a letter to Tonks in 1905, Steer commented that initially he was none too enamoured with the countryside at Chepstow, finding too many high walls and trees, or as Sargent had first dubbed them 'vegetables', interfering with his view, and too many hills to haul himself up. Gradually he must have re-accustomed himself to the scenery, for in a later letter to Behrend he commented on the sentimental feeling he had for that whole area, describing Chepstow itself as 'the plum'. Some of his initial lack of enthusiasm on first visiting the spot may be accounted for by an obviously depressive state of mind, which is reflected in a letter he wrote to Ronald Gray from his lodgings at Wycliffe House:

> The melancholy of a summer's afternoon, the melancholy of many summer's afternoons, weigh upon my soul, and the dismal gloom of the summer holiday is strong within me, for perhaps you don't realise that we say and do the same things in the same way and at the same time every blessed day of our lives . . .

This is an indication of that great sensitivity to his surroundings which in this case doubtless sparked off memories of his childhood, and which implies also the sense of isolation that appears to have swept over him at times. But these recurrent depressive moods were not overwhelming and were largely dealt with via the concentrated activity of his painting, an activity which was ultimately, as he later said himself, the only thing of real value to him.

The four paintings of the castle at Chepstow which resulted from the summer visit did much to establish the growing reputation already referred to. The most successful was apparently painted from the exact position as Turner's painting, looking up towards the castle from the banks on the other side of the Wye. However some doubt exists here. In the MacColl archives is a letter from Chepstow County Council which states that that particular view was impossible, being totally obscured by a large number of sturdy oaks. Turner's picture is the more delicate, and is handled with more subtlety, the castle receding into the evening light with calm skies above. The idyllic pastoral mood is heightened here by the group of cattle on the near bank of the river, and by the figures bathing in the warm waters. By contrast Steer's version is bolder and more directly treated, painted with the midday sun behind the castle creating a *contre jour* effect, with less variation and depth across the canvas, and with the shimmering white clouds associated more with Constable. Steer's paint is much denser, with palette knife and brushmarks more in evidence than in Turner's. Beyond the influence of Turner and Constable, however, continue the Impressionist colour effects that extend throughout his landscape pictures from the previous decades. So, although at first sight the painting seems to be solely concerned with Turner, in fact it combines a number of diverse stylistic influences, giving a vision of landscape which is finally Steer's own.

In a group of pictures from these years up to 1910, Steer began to display an increasing tendency to paint the open vistas most associated with his later works. These birds eye views, where the artist surveys a predominantly unpeopled landscape, were characteristic of much landscape painting of the time. J.D. Innes, for example, was to produce similarly open views of the Welsh countryside around 1910. With Steer this marked a development away from the *sous bois* paintings of oak trees at Knaresborough, and from enclosed pastoral scenes such as *The Embarkment*, towards a much broader vision, a larger view of the lay of the land. There were fewer representations of a specific place or monument, and instead an expression of landscape itself. These new images constitute a turning away from rustic scenery and the picturesque. But the larger concern with topography still retained a sense of personal meaning, the reflective association which in some instances takes on almost abstract or universal values. In this Constable again can be seen as a parallel case, whose early work also veered between the picturesque and the topographical. Steer can be seen then not only to be interested in varying his technical style, but also in the wider issue of modes of representation.

One of the earliest examples of work in this vein, after the *Ludlow Castle* of 1898, is *Rainbow Landscape*, painted in 1901 on his first trip to Bridgnorth in Shropshire. He obviously favoured this site, for he returned there often in subsequent years, and Girtin and Turner had also painted the area in the early nineteenth century. Steer's view here is taken looking down across the wide landscape from the high vantage point of the town. Rain has ceased, and the stormy clouds recede into the background, revealing the double rainbow. There is a clear connection with Rubens' *Rainbow Landscape* here. References to Constable's atmospheric landscapes also abound, in both subject and technique, in this work, and in several others of these years such as in *The Valley of the Severn*, 1902, where the sun bursts through the leaden skies. Like Constable and Turner, Steer was attempting in these pictures to present a fixed image of nature in its extremes of mood and changefulness — the essence of the British climate. Atmosphere is the key to these works, and, as we have seen, the term appears time and time again in contemporary criticism. Interpretations of 'atmosphere' were a prerequisite in depictions of the British landscape, or to 'Englishness' in art throughout this period. Interestingly, in 1902 Roger Fry was also using this term and was writing optimistically of Steer's potential, hoping that "he would be able to express with greater intensity his finely poetic feeling for landscape and atmospheric effect" (RF 1902 656).

Fry, who in general wrote supportively of Steer around this time, must have seen possibilities in his ability to extract the essential abstract qualities in the landscape, to rise beyond the mundane transcription of the scenery and the mild Impressionistic effects. It was a view of Steer shared by several others. The very early 1900s were viewed, even by C. Collins Baker in 1909, as a transitional period, between the more sombre works of the late 1890s and his 'highest point' later the following decade. Still he found the works of the preceding few years as having extraordinary brilliance, also noting the near visionary quality in *The Valley of the Severn* (or *Golden Valley*) that Fry had hinted at.

In these works, and in others from these years — notably from his final visit to Richmond and Hawes in 1903, and others such as

The Storm – Horses Running, 1903 — Steer achieved an effect of real intensity in his depiction of extremes of weather, his often powerful use of colour and the thickly applied, energetic brushmarks. The impact of these paintings is such as to place them far above the weaker efforts of many British adherents of Impressionism. With their strength and immediacy, claims that he acted merely as a *pasticheur* of Turner and Constable seem wholly inadequate. A strong sense of personal inspiration and emotional investment emanate from pictures of this period. This was clearly the quality that Fry discerned, and hoped to encourage in his criticism when he urged Steer to extend further his own "powers of invention".

Within the traditional landscape convention and the overall design of the paintings, a large measure of self-expression is present. In *The Storm – Horses Running*, Bruce Laughton noted a coincidental resemblance to Kandinsky's *Blue Horsemen*, painted one year earlier (BL 1971 93). Such a relationship to the expressionist painter is interesting, for it recalls the earlier resemblance between Steer's watching girls and similar conventions within Symbolism. But ultimately whether Steer borrowed consciously or unconsciously in these cases is actually not the point, because in both instances the strength of the paintings lies in the way in which his own obsessional nature reveals itself.

As Fry himself was doubtless aware, in landscapes as charged and expressive as these, Steer's potential went far beyond the limited capacities of his companions. In this respect the work of Tonks, for example, in spite of his forceful personality, appear simply tame and tasteful. However admirable Tonks' technical skills, the strong feeling of a scientist's observation of natural form excludes any sense of personal involvement with his subject and this deadens his impact, producing an effect similar to Steer's own weaker domestic interior studies. But it was possible to perceive in Steer's landscapes qualities which surpassed the claims and prescriptions made by the domineering clique that surrounded him. In looking at Steer's work in the context of his group of friends, the impression that association with him was ultimately more beneficial for Tonks than for Steer is strengthened. MacColl, who in 1906 was less involved in writing and more with his new post as Keeper of the Tate, was, it seems, content to view Steer purely as the worthy successor to Turner and Constable —

upholder of the intrinsic qualities of a British sensibility. As will be seen, his criticism is essentially very limited after this time.

After a series of successful showings at the NEAC, in 1904 and 1906 in particular, and another one-man exhibition at the Goupil Gallery in 1909, this view of Steer's achievement was so widespread that it began to appear clichéd and hackneyed towards the end of the decade. At this point also a fair amount of self-congratulation went on amongst Steer's clique. George Moore was, needless to say, the loudest in this respect. After flattering reviews from the Goupil show, Moore wrote to Steer reminding him that he was one of his oldest friends and how, since his early visits to Addison Road: "I think I always knew that you were a great painter". Similar sycophancies followed.

In 1906 Steer made a third visit to Ludlow, which in terms of his own tastes and concerns, was a perfect site for him. The town itself, with substantial amounts of early building, its fine castle ruins, its position within the bend of the river Teme and the types of surrounding landscape — all would appeal to Steer. A whole series of views of a favourite spot on Ludlow Walks, overlooking the river and its bridge, resulted from this visit (for example, *Children Playing in a Park, Ludlow*) and the earlier one in 1989–9. All were painted from the same vantage point looking down over the broad landscape. In three versions the same subject recurs; an imaginary group of young girls playing in the foreground. In the first picture of 1898 — the most detailed of the three — the girls are accompanied by a dog which jumps up beside one of the dancing figures. In the second, another scene of 1906–9, the girls are alone and the treatment of the sky and the rough surface of the paint are more reminiscent of Constable's style. In the last of the series, probably completed in 1909, the scene is the same but the setting is later in the evening, and the handling is smoother and more fluid. All of these are reminiscent of the earlier Walberswick girls, and the atmospheric handling of the last one even more so. The dancing girl in white dress and sash particularly recall the images of the *Girls Running on Walberswick Pier* from the late 1880s. This recurrent theme, the consistently repeated images of youth and the lost world of innocence, refers back to the abrupt end to his own ideal childhood, carried on into his later work but with the additional personal association of being set in the large open landscapes that he had known from his earliest years. So the two consistent preoccupations unite in these three paintings. With the changing technique and handling of each Steer looked for ways to achieve the most direct painterly expression of his "sentimental feelings". It was, in effect, via an almost unconscious empathy with Steer's paintings of his own experience — the scenes of his own childhood — that his work developed such appeal. Of course the criticism of the time was not in a position to explore such possibilities, but it was an identification of the individual and strong sense of personal association with the British landscape that was undoubtedly visible in Steer's work to the contemporary audience.

In these years of an ever increasing sense of national and social insecurity, the consistent unease over cultural identity and class relations spawned countless examples of artistic and literary tendencies towards private introspection, played out for example in these idealised visions of the English landscape. The countryside could function not only as a broad-based nationalistic refuge, as previously described, but also as a very personal escape. The particular connotations that Steer's paintings held for himself, and the special sense of melancholy which he experienced on revisiting the scenes of his youth emerged as a pattern amongst artists and in other areas of the arts. The area along the Welsh Borders — Shropshire in particular — had developed a tradition of writers who viewed that specific landscape through personal images of loss. A.E. Housman's *A Shropshire Lad* of 1896 is the best example — the "blue remembered hills" were a "Land of lost content". And Mary Webb's is a later example of a vision which was based on a more private level of meaning, an intensely personal interpretation of the past and the countryside. This sensibility develops particularly amongst artists in the years immediately after the First World War, but its roots lie in the period of the 1900s. Steer is an especially interesting case in this respect, and his Ludlow paintings with their personal symbolism are a prime example.

The imperialist ideologies which resulted in calls for a renewal of art born out of a great national tradition account for a certain amount of the praise for Steer's art. But the more private reflection in his work, the sense of nostalgia for his own individual roots, in a sense relate to a change of spirit. As Martin Wiener has commented, the long and humiliating process of defeat in the Boer War dampened imperialist rhetoric and led to more contemplative forms of introspection. Wiener adds that by the Edwardian period many were arguing that imperialism had "betrayed the 'true' England". And this was essentially the ethos of the 'Little Englanders' (MW 1985 58).

One striking phenomenon of this period, and possibly one of the most powerful effects of the Boer War, was the widening of already existing divisions among the middle classes. The newer and aspiring sections were, for the most part, steadfast in their patriotism, out of a sense of duty and longstanding support for the Empire. Their response was simply increased jingoism. The more traditional elements were more ambivalent. Those who made up the Little Englanders largely condemned British action and were pro-Boer. George Moore found "great spiritual significance" in his pro-Boerism, and stated, possibly fancifully, that it was due to his loathing for the war that he removed himself to Dublin. For Moore, and without doubt for many others, this apparently political stance was perhaps no more than a renewed outburst of class superiority and distaste for the philistines. But it is interesting that his response should have been to depart from London, whatever his purported motives had been. And Steer was doing what he always did, keeping a low profile, reconsidering his private landscapes and his personal symbolism. Martin Wiener's description of the flavour of much contemporary literature as a "blend of idyll and anxiety" (MW 1985 53) seems also a strikingly apt description of Steer at that moment.

1909 was a year of some significance for Steer. In his biography, MacColl cited it as the point at which the "top of the hill was reached" (DSM 1945 51). Steer entered the National Collection with *Chepstow Castle*. The Tate Gallery Trustees apparently "gulped, but swallowed" and accepted the work from its then owner, Mary Hoadley Dodge. The Goupil exhibition held in the same year was, as already mentioned, soundly applauded. The response to the show offers a useful indication of Steer's standing. Friends were unstinting in their praise. William Rothenstein, like Moore, wrote to tell him how much he had always admired his work:

you always seem to me a sort of magician . . . The vitality of your
pictures is magnificent . . . there is a splendid sense of blooms and
health and bursting life about everything you do that fills me with
joy (DSM 1945 52).

Charles Holmes' review in *The Times* on 22 April offered a more
balanced view. Initially Holmes was put off by the way unfinished
pictures had also been included, and urged the visitor to
concentrate on the more "important and ambitious" works.
Highest amongst these he placed *Corfe Castle*, painted from Steer's
visit to Dorset the previous year. It was the largest picture in the
exhibition, and Holmes immediately ranked it alongside Constable
six-footers such as *Salisbury from the Meadows*, a "heroic subject
on a heroic scale". The castle itself is a relatively minor note, set
amidst a sunburst in the centre of a vast overall design of the
sweeping landscape of the Purbeck Hills, with their dark shadows
and the heavy brooding skies above. All detail is subordinate to the
total effect created by the thick layers of oil paint rapidly laid down
with brush and palette knife. For Holmes, Steer's vision is more
forceful, more abstract than Constable's with an accidental quality,
the "vivid pitch of nature herself". On an equal footing Holmes
placed *The Lime Kiln*, painted on the same visit to Corfe, and *The
Balcony*. This last, of 1909, was a painting of Lilian Montgomery
sat in profile idly spinning a globe in front of the large drawing
room window in Cheyne Walk, with its rather Whistlerian view of
Battersea Power Station in the distance. Holmes compared this
work to the Dutch painters Vermeer and De Hooch, but he had
some reservations about the use of so large a scale for such a slight
subject. However he recognised that the size corresponded to the
handling, the strong and summary brushwork. These were the
three most impressive works in the exhibition for Holmes, and
interestingly two of them, *The Balcony* and *Corfe Castle* were
bought by Hugh Lane for the National Collection, Johannesburg.
Geoffrey Blackwell also emerged as an important patron for Steer as
a result of visiting the Goupil show.

The bulk of Holmes' article was devoted to spotting influences
and pointing out similarities with older painters — Rembrandt and
Claude in one instance, Crome and Daubigny in another. A
reference to Watts was even made in connection with *On the
Pierhead*, which for Holmes represented a lighter vein in Steer

which "can descend to mere prettiness" — a fairly typical view of Steer's earlier work at that point. Inevitable references to Turner emerge in relation to *The Isle of Purbeck*, in its colour and atmosphere. Assertions of 'Englishness' began early in the article: "a typically English, 'poetical' sentiment for certain moods of nature . . . a peculiarly lyrical charm", etc, etc. But then an intensity of conviction is noted, and an "almost primitive naiveté of presentment". Yet beyond these descriptive passages little insight into his motivation is offered. Inevitably, as one would expect, Holmes ended by citing Steer as comparable to the "greatest names in English landscape", and the exhibition as final proof that "in him England possesses a really living master of landscape and figure painting".

The kinds of observations made by Holmes and others of his generation are never entirely satisfactory, doing no more than suggesting affiliations and describing tendencies. The peculiar qualities in Steer's art that account for its appeal within a particular audience at a specific moment can perhaps only begin to be understood at a distance. The writings of his friends and critics are useful with hindsight, but are too partisan to be taken literally. Steer's popularity amongst that group is essentially tied up with the experiences, prejudices and preoccupations, however unconsciously felt, of the time.

Steer's position from the late nineteen hundreds was secure — venerated by the majority of critics and certainly no longer perceived by them to be harbouring any modernist European tendencies. One writer expresses this view in describing his work after 1910 as rather a "refined survival from the nineteenth century . . . than as a contribution to the development of art in the twentieth . . ." (C. Harrison 1981 22). His only role in the growth of modern art in Britain is seen to lie in his position as teacher at the Slade school, where the great majority of British modernist painters from the first half of the century trained. Some reference to Steer's reputation there has already been made, and he invariably appears in biographies of these subsequent painters as a lovable eccentric with a rare and instinctive gift in painting.

But from the mid 1900s Steer was increasingly seen by younger artists as belonging to an older established group of artists both at the Slade and amongst the membership of the NEAC, whose numbers continued to swell from the ranks of the Slade. Frank Rutter has noted how, by the turn of the century, a split within the NEAC was already apparent between the 'old guard' who were loyal to Steer, and the 'young guard' who clustered around Augustus John: "Steer was king, without argument, but John was decidedly the Prince of Wales" (FR 1933 88). MacColl was also seen in terms of the old guard — but more disparagingly. One writer described him as a pensioner in a home for art critics.

The review of the December exhibition of the NEAC in the Athenaeum in 1906 pointed to the developing conservatism there, and the writer noted a constant need for new blood in societies which inevitably tended towards small coteries of artists, friends and dependents. The obvious reference to Steer's circle becomes explicit later in the review:

> It will come as a shock to some people to think that virtually for upwards of twenty years Mr Wilson Steer has been on the Hanging Committee that hung his own pictures. No Academician could say so much . . . such a position has its dangers. Mr Steer sometimes nods, and when he does his defects are paraded as virtues (Ath 1906 865).

This writer looked to Sickert, newly arrived from Dieppe, to inject some of the old spirit of controversy into the Club. Sickert's return had been the cause of much speculation amongst the various cliques, for his opinion could never be safely prejudged. His subsequent involvements with ex-Slade students Gore, Gilman and Rutherston, and the formation of the Fitzroy Street Group in 1907 and later the Camden Town group only increased the isolation of Steer's circle from developing mainstream debate. Within these new factions and with Frank Rutter's Allied Artists' Association exhibition in 1909, the enthusiastic atmosphere for more recent European art heightened amongst younger artists and Steer, MacColl, Tonks and Brown appeared more and more out of date.

In 1909 Orpen exhibited his *Homage to Manet* at the NEAC, and it appears almost as a final summation of a particular period in British painting. The picture showed Steer along with MacColl, Tonks, Sickert and Hugh Lane seated round a table below Manet's portrait of *Eva Gonzalez*, listening to George Moore deliver his memoirs of the Impressionists. Sickert manages a straight face, and Steer wears his resigned and stoical expression. From this point on the opinions and prejudices of the most vocal around that table — Sickert excluded — appeared to belong to another age. In the years preceding Roger Fry's first Post-Impressionist exhibition any critical affinities between himself and MacColl ebb away. MacColl's post at the Tate was accompanied by seats on various committees, such as the National Art Collection Fund, and the Contemporary Art Society. In 1911 he left the Tate to become Keeper of the Wallace Collection. His health was poor at that time and this was felt to be a less demanding position. During these years he was to become something of a guardian of English heritage and values, an acknowledged arbiter of taste. Sickert described the situation succinctly in the *New Age* in 1910: "D.S. MacColl talks about the 'tyranny of the Academy'. I am not so sure if he doesn't propose to give us King Stork himself instead" (WS 1910 65).

The estrangement between Fry and MacColl grew out of MacColl's complete inability to come to terms with French painting after Manet and Degas. And yet the tendency to write Steer off at this point as a spent force is ill-judged. There are qualities in his work subsequently which, while not overtly progressive, nevertheless display an urge to continue the exploration of his medium and to adopt new approaches that in many respects distanced him from the steadily retrogressive opinions of his peer group, certainly from Tonks and MacColl.

III

1910–1942

A Last Brush With Modernism

Between 1905 and 1914 a series of exhibitions gradually initiated the gallery-visiting public and enthusiastic younger art students into more recent developments in French painting. The diversity of styles from Cezanne to Matisse was conveniently categorised as Post-Impressionist by Fry at his Grafton Galleries show at the end of 1910. But some measure of critical debate had already developed prior to Fry's exhibition. One early showing, also at the Grafton Galleries, was Durand-Ruel's exhibition in 1905 which contained ten paintings by Cezanne. Immediate opinion on this painter in particular was hostile. George Moore felt his work represented "the anarchy of painting . . . art in delirium" (GM 1906 35), and Frank Rutter puzzled as to what "these funny brown and olive landscapes" (FR 1933 111-14) were doing in an Impressionist exhibition.

Other showings of Post-Impressionist art followed with the International Society exhibition in 1908 and, as mentioned, Rutter's Allied Artists Association in 1909. Another significant exhibition held that same year in Brighton contained a section on recent French art including Cezanne, Van Gogh, Matisse and other Fauve painters. So the public were generally aware of these developments before 1910. Journals like *The Studio* and, from Fry's appointment as editor, *The Burlington Magazine*, published reviews on the development of French art in these years also. Newspapers gave considerable attention to the 'new movement' whose radical appeal made it eminently newsworthy. In 1908 the critic of *The Times* — pointing to the growing conservatism amongst supposedly avant garde British painting — commented that those who continued to feel that NEAC exhibitions were in any sense revolutionary, should go to Paris, where the most advanced of British painting would appear: "as timid as the opinion of a Fabian socialist compared with those of a bomb-throwing anarchist" (*The Times* 1908 8).

The constant references to anarchy — the implied connection between modern French painting and political anarchism — were used consistently by the more reactionary critics as a means of drawing public attention to the dangerous threat of Post-Impressionism, to traditional techniques and traditional ways of looking at art. Faced with labour unrest at home and some anarchist activity, and with the constant press reports of revolutionary acts in Europe, intimations such as these were bound to be effective. Alongside those, implications of mental deficiency or affected pretentiousness were the mainstay of hostile attacks. Often the tone of much earlier criticisms of Steer can be reheard — the suggestion of "midsummer madness", "sheer unnaturalness" etc.

Just as the early British supporters of Impressionism attempted to convince audiences here of the traditional and therefore respectable roots of the movement, so too did the allies of the Post-Impressionists. Popular conceptions of this supposedly new movement were that it was a rejection of and a reaction against the aesthetic ideals of its predecessor, and that its aim was pure nihilism. The response by Fry and other early supporters, was to describe post-Impressionism as having firm historical antecedents, and further as bringing a spirit of renewal to contemporary art which had become increasingly dull and repetitive. So pictures by Cezanne, Van Gogh, Gauguin and Matisse were described as providing a liberating freedom from constraints that were also based on traditions in art that stretched far beyond the nineteenth century conventions upheld by their many critics. For the latter the crudeness and the unnaturalistic representation were anathema to established tastes.

Fry attempted to convince viewers that the crudeness and lack of obvious naturalism was nothing new, and was a common characteristic of pre-Renaissance art; and secondly that it was grounded in a specific aesthetic. Post-Impressionist paintings, he argued, addressed the imagination directly, not via strict adherence to natural forms but because of their capacity to appeal an the imaginative and contemplative life. This was a concept that developed out of the late nineteenth century theory of expression in art — that art is a language which communicates meaning to the individual through forms and colours with which he or she has some instinctive empathy, rather than through literal descriptions of reality.

Seen in this light it seems not a great distance from MacColl's own principles. He had long campaigned for a view of art that was not tied to pure representation and had endlessly acknowledged the expressive power of painting itself, divorced from mere illustration. He had even, like Fry, been deeply influenced by Tolstoy's *What is Art?* when it appeared in 1898. Tolstoy was especially influential in the developing view of art's expressive and communicative functions, and with Fry, MacColl saw the book as a "pointer in aesthetics". But Fry took the theory to its extremes, in MacColl's view, and the painters he upheld in this respect were beyond reasonable comprehension.

That earlier description of MacColl's critical perceptions as ultimately limited remains the most apt. In previous years he had shared some of the terminology that Fry developed into his own critical language. The word 'rhythm' is significant in this sense. MacColl had frequently discussed its importance as a constructive element in a painting, inherent within the forms and handling, not superimposed onto the surface. The term rhythm was used constantly by younger artists and critics in discussions on modern French art and culminated in the publication of a magazine of that name from 1911, directly related to the latest developments in painting seen in Paris.

MacColl's use of the term appears vague in these later contexts, and despite his critical statements the signs of a premeditated concern with overly refined and superficially elegant arrangements are easily detectable in his own watercolours and architectural drawings. Steer himself had found that MacColl's painting tended to be too tasteful. The rhythm, the echoes of gesture never emerged with the simultaneous spontaneity that he admired in other art. In his own case preoccupation with rhythm appears simply as overtly displayed style, extrinsic not intrinsic to the work. In an article in *The Studio* in 1945 MacColl described Fry as the pied piper of the cranks. And for many years he continued to attack Fry's work in this manner, in spite of their private friendship. Fry himself withstood these criticisms with considerable calm. In a letter written in 1922 he acknowledged that they regarded each other as "misguided in aesthetic judgements", adding that, "I don't take it to heart when you say that my pictures are the utterly dismal performance of a theory-ridden painter".

While it is perhaps understandable that MacColl should have had little taste for the art that Fry supported, his total lack of insight into those paintings is quite astonishing. Cezanne, for example, he describes as "a painter who had a true gift of colour, but by defect of eyesight lost a never secure sense of form". A quite ludicrous assessment. At the time of Fry's first Post-Impressionist exhibition MacColl was ill and his critical reaction didn't appear until two years later, in an article entitled 'A Year of Post-Impressionism', by which time, as he put it, the "new religion [was] established, the old gods . . . bundled without ceremony into the lumber room" (JBB 1988 264). At some length he disputed claims that Cezanne was a 'classic' and stated that essentially his touch was impressionist and lacking the formal constructive logic that would earn him that title.

In Gauguin MacColl found nothing revolutionary, only the drawing of Degas, yet stiffer and less flexible. Van Gogh he compared to Blake, yet without the 'mental range' and 'endurance' of the latter. MacColl was effectively engaged in this article in pulling his own particular gods back out of the lumber room. And yet in spite of his consistent disparaging of Post-Impressionism, in general a more favourable public response began to outweigh bad criticism, and his own position was increasingly isolated. From his death in 1907 Cezanne was the subject of endless debate and controversy, such that Steer and Tonks, grown weary at the constant sound of his name, re-named him Mr Harris. However there is evidence that Steer took more serious note of Cezanne's painting.

Steer's utterances on the subject of Post-Impressionism are, needless to say, few and far between. His single comment on leaving the first Grafton exhibition, which he toured in silence, was allegedly: "Well I suppose they all have private incomes". By this he may also have been remembering his own position at the time of his more daring technical experiments in the early 1890s. Some interest in Cezanne's earlier work, possibly encouraged by his friendship with Fry at this time, is apparent in work produced from a trip to France in 1907, his first visit for thirteen years and also his last. Primarily this was a painting expedition to Montreuil, but

Steer also travelled to Paris and visited the Cezanne memorial exhibition at Le Salon d'Automne. MacColl records Steer's visit to that exhibition and re-uses his own phrase about Cezanne's "never secure sense of form". He says nothing about Steer's verdict other than that Steer had been struck by the early still life of the Black Clock — which MacColl himself admired. So he continues to present Steer in his own prescriptive manner.

According to MacColl, Steer's affection for the site of his *Outskirts of a Town* was based on a "clump of old, unpollarded trees that might have been English, reminiscent of Shaftesbury". This is the sum of MacColl's description of the work. He went on to describe the jolly activities of 'the three' and their companion Ronald Gray, mentioning an apparent flirtation between Steer and an American student that ended abruptly on an invitation to meet the woman's parents later in London — to the great relief, it appears, of his friends (DSM 1945 86-7).

The painting MacColl referred to is one of three versions, known collectively as *Montreuil from the Ramparts*. In all three the diagonal slope of the largest tree trunk is echoed by the direction of the other trees. These set up a rhythmic force across the canvas that is a particular feature of Cezanne's paintings. It has been suggested that these paintings, which were for the most part produced on the spot, were worked on later and presumably after Steer's visit to the exhibition in Paris; therefore some indirect or even specific influence is not inconceivable. The paintwork itself is so densely impasted that, as a result, some of the surface areas take on abstract qualities — which again might imply some reference to Cezanne. Although all this is conjecture, there are certainly indications that Steer took more personal note of the French artist than MacColl would care to admit.

In one other painting from this Montreuil visit, the *Grande Place* — a frontal view of the vast town square — the low and narrow band of buildings shrinks into the lower half of the canvas, dominated by the large expanse of the sky. The strong formal composition of the work was later noted by Roger Fry who, writing to Steer, said that he "found the relation of the sky to the buildings and the foreground one of those discoveries of proportion that only very real artists make". So Steer's paintings of this period represent the high point for Fry, the point at which he perceived qualities most in tune with his own ideals. This explains his great disappointment with works like *The End of the Chapter*, in which Steer appeared to have been swayed by Tonks' judgement and domineering influence.

The combination of Steer's impressionable character and his natural desire to avoid unnecessary aggravation, meant that he was increasingly disinclined to upset the opinion of his sometimes overbearing cronies. There is always a conflict in Steer between this innate conservatism, the desire to leave things as they are, and a more adventurous and independent spirit that, in earlier times especially, led him to take risks with his painting. In later years the conservative element was the most dominant certainly, but there are indications, with these Montreuil paintings as specific examples, that without the protective restraints of his friends he may have experimented more freely with elements of contemporary French art — though more from technical curiosity than from any philosophical or theoretical position. In spite of the conflicting aspects of his personality he remained consistently averse to any intellectualising or to any debate over the 'meaning' of art and how to interpret pictures. Steer painted a scene simply because he found it attractive or because it interested him from a technical point of view. Anything else was an irrelevance. He was friendly with Fry purely on a personal level, and certainly not through any concern for Fry's theories on modern art. The friendship cooled however when Fry resigned from the NEAC and suggested that Steer should do the same. This constituted a lack of loyalty to Steer and he refused.

The interest in stylistic elements of Cezanne's art that may be inferred from the Montreuil paintings was a brief interlude for Steer, and was succeeded by the pictures of Corfe and the bend of the Severn in which Turner and Constable emerge as the main influence, as already discussed. These paintings were exhibited at NEAC exhibitions in 1909 and 1910 and they formed the basis of his reputation for the following decade.

After 1910 these kinds of landscapes predominated, and with the growing number of watercolours in his output, Steer's handling became increasingly fluid and spontaneous. His use of this medium at a time of developing modernism in British painting prior to the war further distanced him from the preoccupations of his students at the Slade. In these tumultuous years when younger artists were declaring their allegiances to either the decorative abstraction of the Bloomsbury ilk, or the fervent dynamism of the Vorticists, Steer was painting cloud conditions and sunsets at Porchester and Harwich, his painting sites for 1912 and 1914 respectively.

These sites marked a shift in focus from inland scenes of rivers and valleys to a renewed interest in the sea and coast which he had not tackled since his Walberswick and Boulogne/Etaples excursions. Unlike the earlier work these are largely unpeopled and he concentrates on harbours and estuaries and the sailing boats. Scenes such as these, painted for the most part in watercolour, reflect Turner's later work, but also signal a return to Monet and to a Whistlerian approach — the handling is slight, shapes and objects are suggested and unnecessary detail eliminated. The aim is overall atmospheric effect. Watercolour gave him a route out of the heavy impasto that was a characteristic of so many of his oil paintings. Yet in one sense a similarity exists — the thick paint of his oils, as noted, was so extreme in some instances that it was almost autonomous and not merely illustrative. In the watercolours the same process occurs — gradually the mistiness, the sparseness of natural detail and the liquid fluidity of the brushstrokes leads in the same direction. It is as if Steer's fascination with the potential of the medium develops such that the subject becomes almost secondary on occasions. It is a vision much removed from the grand, evocative and picturesque landscapes of Yorkshire and the Welsh Borders from around the mid-1900s. Some, John Rothenstein for example, have described it as a shift from an 'epic' to a 'lyrical' mood (JR 1952 74). Yet with the similarities just pointed out there seems to me to be a large degree of consistent preoccupation nonetheless.

The watercolours Steer produced in this period around the first world war are impressionist in the strictest sense of the term. And he perfected the technique rapidly in these years. MacColl has provided an interesting account of Steer's practice of working in this area:

> Seated on a sketching stool he held the folio well away between his knees or feet, and from a colour box of hard cakes on his left thumb and an ample fully charged sable in his right, he spread the tones and struck in the accents that became broader and more decisive, with emptier scenes, as time went on: an affair of

atmosphere and space, mass and umbrage of clouds and trees, horizontals of sea, punctuated and given recession by a few barges or other foreground shapes. He won what I have called a 'Chinese-like' control in the placing, shape and subtle modulation of the wash, between damp and dry of the paper (DSM 1945 113).

For a while after 1914, Steer's expeditions to the coast ceased primarily as a result of the conditions of war and naval activity. In the early summer of 1915 he travelled instead to Painswick in Gloucestershire — a return to his old haunts with views over the Severn Valley and the Welsh Hills from the top of Painswick Beacon. So Steer revisited his familiar landscapes at the outbreak of war. Later he was joined by Brown and Ronald Gray, and was happily ensconced for the remainder of that summer, painting in a converted iron shed. According to his acquaintance C.M. Gere, who arranged much of his visit, Steer became something of a landmark during the stay, sat on a low stool up on the hill, a rotund and almost immobile form.

At this point in his mid-fifties Steer had clearly become something of a caricature to all who knew him. His personality appeared as the sum of his accumulated idiosyncrasies. Without doubt he consciously cultivated this persona; it could prove a convenient escape mechanism in particular circumstances and generally made everyday life easier for him. From these years onwards he rarely ventured outside his habitual circle of like-minded painters and critics — mostly middle-aged, confirmed bachelors. His contacts with people from social classes or backgrounds unlike his own were extremely limited.

One exception, however, occurred in 1916 when he was commissioned to paint Chirk Castle in Shropshire by its then owner Lord Howard de Walden. Steer spent several weeks staying at Chirk. It was the only castle he painted that was still inhabited, and he therefore found himself amidst the aristocracy. He appears, from letters, to have thoroughly enjoyed the lifestyle, the weekend house parties, practical jokes and so on, and the complete contrast to his usual company. His eccentricities and rather bizarre appearance endeared him to the family and their guests. In a letter, de Walden later remembered how the company, for the most part "young and riotous and far from artistic", were "all devoted to Steer, although they did tease him about his greatcoat". Apart from difficulties of getting down to work Steer found that life at the castle "passes like a pleasant dream" and found Chelsea dull in comparison on his return: "my home seems to have contracted, but I got a warm welcome from my Nanny and the tom cat", he wrote to Lady de Walden (DSM 1945 89-91).

The stay at Chirk resulted in at least nine views of the castle and its surroundings and a portrait of Lady de Walden in loose flowing dress reclining in an armchair. MacColl pointed out the interesting parallel between Steer's relation to Chirk and its owner and Turner's position at Petworth some hundred years earlier. This scrves to highlight his separation not simply from contemporary artistic debate in London, but also from social conditions at the time.

The First World War seems to have impinged little on his consciousness, in its early years at least. And, as suggested, his return to his native countryside, his excursion into the timeless, leisurely existence of the aristocracy, were perhaps a deliberate avoidance of the issue.

A direct involvement with the war arose however in 1918 when he was commissioned as a War Artist, at which point he produced some of his most successful work of the period. The experience of war had enormous impact on the direction of painting in Britain and on the subsequent lives and attitudes of large numbers of young artists. Although a section refused participation and declared themselves pacifists — as for example did many of Fry's personal friends and associates of Bloomsbury — for the most part Steer's students at the Slade joined in the patriotic fervour that accompanied the onset of war. Several of their number joined active service in the Artists Rifles — later described as a "scruffy lot of painters, sculptors, actors, musicians, hairdressers, sceneshifters etc" (JL 1940 139). Alongside these, the aggressive and ultimately fascistic ideologies of avant garde groups like Wyndham Lewis and C.R. Nevinson's Vorticists welcomed the opportunities of war; its violence and dynamism, its potential for cleansing the old order and establishing the new. Steer would have been horrified by such a prospect.

By 1916, while Steer was in residence at Chirk Castle, a groundswell of opinion mounted in favour of artists being allowed to document action at the front, a campaign led in large degree by

William Rothenstein. Rothenstein had always been ready to swing into action on behalf of some cause or principle. As Steer later commented to Behrend: "Will paints much the same as the rest of us, but from higher motives of course". This campaign stressed artists' potential propaganda value in providing visual information on circumstances in the battlefield, but was intended also to provide the artists themselves with an income for their art which was increasingly difficult to achieve at home. But the younger artists were not alone in their immediate involvement. Steer's acquaintance John Lavery readily, if briefly, joined up, and Tonks was actively engaged from an early stage in the medical corps both as artist and doctor, later specialising in recording cases of plastic surgery, then in its infancy. In 1917 Tonks accompanied Sargent to the Somme. Both produced powerful images of the effects of war with a realist urgency far removed from their pre-war portraits and delicate domestic genre pieces. Along with these a number of NEAC stalwarts as well as friends and acquaintances of Steer involved themselves in depicting the war from its first years. Notably Orpen, who by this point was also a successful portrait painter, was with the Army Service Corps from early 1916, and at the beginning of 1917 left for the Western Front.

Clausen, a founder member of the NEAC with Steer, remained in England but produced lithographs for the 'Britain's Efforts and Ideals — the Great War' exhibition, commissioned for the Ministry of Information, and shown at the Fine Art Society in July 1917. A.S. Hartrick, another of Steer's generation, was also involved in this. But Slade staff and students were particularly favoured as documenters of the war, as a result of their continued tradition of technical skill and sound draughtsmanship. Steer's participation in the final year came when he was commissioned by the British War Memorials Committee (BWMC) to produce a series of paintings of Dover Harbour — this was part of the scheme for pictures of war activities at home intended for what became the Imperial War Museum. The BWMC had commissioned a number of artists to work along the South Coast to document naval activities and had particularly high hopes of Steer in this respect. Such was his reputation in the established art world that they looked for a "great national possession" (M & SH 1983 111).

So Steer returned again to the coastal scenes he had been interested in from 1912. According to MacColl this assignment was a happy choice for him, he was consistently critical of the old Army Command but had a profound love and admiration for the Navy. His happiness was shortlived, however, for his assignment meant experiences of the wartime conditions he had avoided thus far. Letters to his friends are full of characteristic complaints about the levels of discomfort he had to endure on his arrival at Dover. The BWMC scheme provided basic expenses for materials and accommodation, but as such standards were fairly low. Steer found his hotel "both depressing and sloppy" and soon found another one where: ". . . the food being excellent . . . it is quite likely that ere long I may regain my lost figure", he wrote to Blackwell. A typical letter for Steer: first describing living conditions, then the weather, and his work last. The Admiralty Pier in Dover, his chosen position, was vast, with apparently no shelter from the 'gales', although this was July, and he went on: ". . . all the permissions and restrictions seem to have a paralysing influence and at times I feel I cannot bear it, especially when I have done a bad watercolour, which occurs all too frequently". In a letter to Ronald Gray the following month he described the slow progress of his work, his downhearted state and the fact that "whenever I sit down to sketch some blighter comes up and wants to see my permit". To make matters worse his landlady had viewed him with great suspicion, and thinking him a spy, went to the police. In late September he was still struggling with his picture, finding ships and boats "obstinate customers to deal with, and after spending much time and labour in putting one in, one finds one has got it in the wrong place" (DSM 1945 92–3).

He produced, with great pains, at least nine canvases from his stay at Dover — the *Dover Harbour*, now in the Imperial War Museum, and another five, one presented by himself in 1919 and four purchased by the Museum with money from a fund set up by Muirhead-Bone. 'The Bone Fund' was intended to raise the standard of 'official art'. The *Dover Harbour* he described to Blackwell is painted from the end of the pier, with the castle and cliffs in the distance wedged between the large cloud filled sky above and the choppy seas below. The nettings, harbour defences and the spray from a launch provided converging movement for

MacColl, who viewed the work as "accurate history and beauty well married".

Following on the success of this work came a commission from the Admiral of the Fleet to paint a scene from the Battle of Jutland. But working from models of ships provided by the Admiralty proved an impossibility for Steer and the finished canvas he sold apparently for the price of the frame. Work for the Admiralty continued throughout the last year of the war, and involved a trip to Rosyth, the naval dockyard on the Firth of Forth near Edinburgh. This was his only visit to Scotland and he stayed with his sister's family in India Street, Edinburgh — visiting galleries, looking for coins and enjoying the company of his family and their friends before embarking on a grossly uncomfortable wartime train journey back to London. Thereafter his excursions were strictly limited to the South of England, and increasingly to the coast.

The year after the war Steer revisited the Isle of Wight. In 1892 he had painted his series of pictures of the boats at Cowes, but in 1919 he travelled to Alum Bay at which point he returned to the approach to harbour and estuary subjects that he had dealt with in watercolours just prior to 1914. He chose similar sites for most of the 1920s and throughout these years the process of abstraction that has already been observed occurred with increased emphasis. Details disappear, and brushmarks are more sweeping and determined until, as he says, the watercolours became "an affair of atmosphere and space". It has been suggested that a re-encounter with Monet's painting in London in 1910 had a considerable influence on the appearance of these watercolours. No longer did they serve simply as preparatory sketches; as Cal Clothier put it, they are "pure drawings" in their own right, and nature is represented in limited tones and harmonies rather than by accumulated fact (CC 1985 27).

The sense in which the abstract qualities of the medium itself gradually supersede literal transcription has been pointed to already. Further than this, however, the way that Steer's earlier use of oil paint acquired something of an expressive life of its own applies in this context as well. Clothier described this tendency when he wrote that ultimately Steer was searching for a method whereby "emotional and spiritual states could be communicated through landscape, where a private response to his subject is expressed through technique and method of representation". This is of course a very central feature of all of Steer's art, emerging most clearly in areas with specific personal meaning for himself — his childhood countryside, but also coastal areas and beach resorts. These always retained a special significance in his oeuvre, and in his own mind, whether peopled as in the Walberswick days, or empty and desolate in watercolours after the war.

The exact importance of these coastal scenes is difficult to determine, for they could not have featured in his own childhood to any degree. But he seemed to have used views of sea and coast almost as an area in which to resolve his own state of mind — happiness, nostalgia, melancholy, even a certain bleakness; all of these conditions have corresponding paintings of coastal subjects, and mood is established primarily through colour, tone and handling, not choice of detail or incident. So in many ways the enterprise of these watercolours from around the 1920s relates to that of his oils from the late 1890s.

The notion of a British landscape (or seascape) as a vehicle for the expression of private emotion gains in currency and is easily discernible in the art of many painters just after the war and throughout the twenties. For younger artists the experiences of being at war concentrated feelings about the essential character of 'Englishness'. There is in much of the art of the period a visible tendency towards viewing the landscape as a touchstone for qualities made more valuable for having been almost lost. This tendency is all the more marked amongst those artists who had gone to war with a determined optimism and a modernist fervour only to find those characteristics quite out of place in relation to the awfulness of their circumstances. In many cases, a damaged personality, like that of Steer's ex-student Paul Nash for example, on his return home was to view his surroundings in terms of his own individual need for safety and a sense of order. This process occurred for many, and in each the landscape acts as a personal metaphor, an arena for private expression, taking shape according to the artist's innermost motivations. So Steer, although his outward experiences were of a totally different kind from those of Nash, for example, was nonetheless approaching art and nature in the same way. It could be argued that Steer had always done this, and that the reason why his watercolours of the twenties appear so advanced in the context of some of his work just prior to these, is that at this point he achieved a mature synthesis of the form and content of his work. This might belie some expectations of him at that date, at the start of his sixties, when many had already written him off as hopelessly conservative and a spent force.

The countryside in general grew in importance as a site for artists in the years just after the war. Even some previously considered urban types joined in with Steer in the annual summer excursions, or else removed themselves completely to rural settings. From the early part of the war Fry's circle, for instance, had largely departed from London to various spots in Sussex and Berkshire, and several of Steer's closer acquaintances moved outwards too. Perhaps if Steer had had a family he may well have done the same, for his summer visits increased in importance to him as the years passed. His reluctance to be completely rusticated, and his continued residence in Chelsea, was, it seems, through habit but also for the contact with those friends who stood for his family. London itself could have given him little pleasure by this time.

The English coast gained the attention of a number of artists during these years. Even artists most noted for their treatment of city subjects dealt with it. Charles Ginner, associated with Sickert and the Camden Town Group, was producing watercolour sketches of the Dorset coastline in 1922. Paul Nash was painting the sea at Dymchurch in Kent almost as a therapeutic exercise following his nervous breakdown. Numerous other artists found varying methods of making personal interpretations of rural scenery. Some, in contrast to Steer, found refuge imagery in small close-up views of the landscape, winding country lanes, leafy gardens and cottages. The open panoramic views that Steer favoured offered no sense of security for these artists, many of whom, such as Graham Sutherland, were attracted by the enclosed sanctuary of nature embodied in the visions of Samuel Palmer, whose paintings were shown in a large exhibition in 1926. This was a different version of 'Englishness' from that of Steer although he perhaps came closest to it in his paintings of oak avenues at Knaresborough and at Ludlow in the early 1890s. But the wide open surveys of the land most associated with Steer are also represented by other artists in the twenties, such as James Macintosh Patrick. But in these cases the scenery, though large, is usually well-ordered and under control. The taste for the crumbling decay of the picturesque emerged in the work of John Piper, as did the love for what MacColl had described as "the old bones of England". Monuments and ancient relics which Steer had long delighted over were regularly treated by artists from the twenties onwards as emblems of permanence and continuity in spite of social disarray. And so in a number of different ways the themes and preoccupations of Steer's landscape art emerge most interestingly in the work of a larger group of artists in the 1920s. An inner response to particular circumstances was being mediated through specific representations of the land.

But an emotional relationship with the countryside was not solely the province of painters. The consistently growing trend for city dwellers to turn out at holiday times and to tour the nation's beauty spots continued apace. This frequently caused irritation for Steer and his painting companions, who grew weary of their presence. The annoyance of inquisitive tourists peering over the shoulder while sketching was a common cause for complaint, and Steer grew ever more intolerant. Much of his planning for painting trips now involved avoidance of the more popular sites, and this led him to explore areas that might initially seem unpromising. The inconvenience that the holidaymakers caused also gave rise to occasional outbursts of overt snobbery. In one instance, on a trip to Bridgnorth in 1925, Steer complained in a letter to Tonks that the "Bank Holiday was rather acute here being within easy reach of Wolverhampton and the proletariat seemed to pervade the town". The search for peaceful places grew more and more difficult: "We go out full of hope and return with our tails between our legs". Since the early nineteen hundreds the number of motor vehicles and later motor buses steadily increased. With the establishment of the Road Board in 1909 and the subsequent construction of many new roads, access to once secluded parts of the country became ever easier. Some general concern for land preservation was in evidence during these years, with organisations like the Society for the Promotion of Nature Reserves from 1912, but still fears over the invasion of the country side both from visitors and new inhabitants continued. Throughout the twenties more societies came into existence which were concerned to safeguard the national heritage from the onslaught of modern progress. The Council for the

121

Protection of Rural England, and another for Rural Wales, emerged at this time.

For Steer and his companions modern progress was quite undesirable, and their letters increasingly reflect this attitude. Their concern was not for the effect of change on the lives of rural communities, but for aesthetic issues alone. The appearance of the landscape was in danger — its timeless quality, the sense of permanence and the reassurance that it offered was under threat. This was a bias that emerged in countless guide books in search of rural England by writers like H.V. Morton, which began to be published in the twenties. A very clear class prejudice pertains here, as with Steer's earlier comment.

In his biography of Steer, MacColl makes remarks typical of the attitudes of his contemporaries when he talks of Steer's experiences at that time:

> Already the 'beauty-spots' of the country were thick-clustered with teashops and cars; walkers were driven from the crowded roads; ribbons of houses blotted out elm rows and pasture; cornfields were derelict; fishing fleets and sailing barges laid up; coasts given over to asphalt, bathing-boxes or pools, 'fun fairs' and bungalows (DSM 1945 168-9).

In other words Steer's traditional subjects were under siege, and MacColl voices the discontent of the cultural critic which began to be heard from the mid-nineteenth century. Steer, whose views were the same, was briefer but to the point: "One half of the world seems to be constantly occupied in mucking up the other", he told Behrend. Places like Corfe Castle, which Steer had rendered with such epic grandeur after the turn of the century, were, some fifteen years later, engulfed according to MacColl by, "coach loads of grossly fed and apathetic tourists [on] the regulation round before their meal". Steer's paintings of these sites seemed all the more precious as a result, and appeared almost as a document of a heritage in danger of destruction.

By the early twenties the longstanding trio of Steer, Brown and Coles had dissolved, and Steer's main painting companions were Ronald Gray and most often George Behrend. Behrend cites Steer's famous lethargy as a motivating factor in his production of watercolours after the first world war. Watercolours, he wrote, "were easy to do and sell and involved no trouble about finding a suitable studio in which to work without draughts and discomforts". This view seems rather uncharitable at first, but he went on to comment that Steer's lethargy was not due to idleness, but because by this stage he was "chronically bronchial and catarrhal".

In the early twenties the two painted together at Brill and Long Crendon in Buckinghamshire. Behrend, in notes written after Steer's death, confirms the daily routines that these painting trips involved, starting work promptly at ten each day except for Sunday when no painting was done. In the evenings the whisky bottle came out after seven and Steer, who never read, occupied himself with chess and a hand of patience before bed. In Long Crendon they rented a house for ten weeks and were looked after by various helpers from the village nearby. In that long, uninterrupted summer of 1924 Steer produced numerous watercolours which epitomised his current tendencies towards large airy skies with notes of detail merely suggested and an overall feel of light and space. By now his technical skills with the medium were at a peak, but the final measure of their worth was still a matter of chance. The pictures, if they worked, were still 'flukes'. That element of uncertainty was clearly part of the attraction for Steer. Watercolour is an area of painting which by its nature minimises theoretical speculation; it requires an intuitive sense of judgement, which Steer definitely possessed. MacColl and Tonks could only wonder at his best achievements; they could certainly not intervene with their advice and opinions. Perhaps this contributed to the appeal of the medium for Steer as well.

In March and April of 1924 he had held his third one-man exhibition at the Goupil Gallery. This exhibition of thirty oils also included over forty of his most recent watercolours, which signifies their growing importance as far as he was concerned. Roger Fry reviewed the show in the *New Statesman* and this review provides interesting comment and a useful indication of Fry's assessment of Steer's achievements as a whole (in DSM 1945 182–3). This was in fact Steer's only substantial showing since his previous Goupil show of 1909, except for regular inclusion at the NEAC. Fry was delighted to see it. He felt it would be instructive for the present generation of painters who knew little of Steer's work, and almost nothing of his earlier Impressionist work — his best period for Fry. He began by paying homage to Steer's instinctive gifts for colour and *mise en page*, his unassuming character and direct singlemindedness. But the lifelong openness to the influence of others he viewed as a weakness, in the way that many later critics were to do also. Like MacColl, however, Fry felt that Steer interpreted Monet's example perfectly, using it to reveal that typically English, poetical sentiment for certain moods of nature that nearly all supporters of Steer described, Charles Holmes being another notable example. Like both of these critics, Fry noted the lyrical charm, but unlike MacColl and Holmes, he felt that Steer never again achieved the intensity of conviction of his pictures of Walberswick and the coastlines of northern France. They had for Fry an "almost primitive naivete of presentment", a quality that he admired in the best of French painting from around the turn of the century.

The "elegance of facture" and the "English love of decorative effect" which followed on from the influence of Monet was less successful in Fry's view. But in the pictures of the 1890s concerned with these decorative aims and with colour harmonies he revealed himself as essentially a very gifted colourist. Finally Fry regretted the organiser's decision not to show his recent work in a separate room because he felt that this suffered by comparison with the brilliance of his earlier pictures, subduing their own remarkable qualities. By these he is referring to the landscapes and watercolours of the previous few years. Here he perceived a return to the effects of the earlier Impressionist work: "in the extreme simplicity of the presentment, the absence of any premeditated approach or search for effective display of the motive", although they were far more understated in terms of colour — subtlety he regarded as an attribute associated with age. These later works were like abbreviated statements for Fry — reduced to a small range of tone and detail but "chosen with such a sense of their significance that they suffice to evoke the effect". Fry ended by pointing to a comparison with some of Matisse's similarly restrained landscapes — both he viewed as Impressionist, but Matisse retained a feeling for form, a solid scaffold of constructive design which for Fry was the one element that was lacking with

Steer, and that hindered the development of his "extraordinary gifts".

There are aspects of Fry's assessment of Steer in which he seems close to MacColl's own opinions, especially in his observation of poetical sentiment and Steer's superb skill at the creation of colour harmonies. But in his ultimate opinions of the most successful periods of his work, his favouring of the early Impressionist paintings in particular, Fry is finally at odds with MacColl, and this eventual parting of the ways on critical matters is a constant feature of their writings. Fry noted it himself in a letter to MacColl of that same year:

> We sometimes get similar impressions from pictures and then suddenly we get not merely different but diametrically opposite ones, so that they are like the concave and convex aspects of a hollow tray.

From the mid-twenties Steer's painting excursions were made increasingly nearer to home. In his constant wish to avoid the ever present hordes of tourists, his choice of sites became more and more unusual. Behrend remarked on this, saying that Steer passed over the obvious painting grounds and liked "mucky places" — unfashionable areas like Whitstable and Harwich. One superficially unpromising place was Shoreham along the coast from Brighton where they painted in 1926. At first view this appeared simply as a collection of the holiday and retirement bungalows for which MacColl had expressed distaste. But with his usual determination Steer found an attractive site by the river. The shoreline, which was overpopulated and lacking a lavatory, was a less convenient site.

By this point Steer was nearing his late sixties and was increasingly unwell, which accounts also for the unadventur-ousness of his expeditions. Yet he surprised his friends by his tenacity. Behrend recounts a surely apocryphal tale of him attempting to swim the Channel: "He started, full of buck, and was in the water exactly two seconds when, owing to the excessive choppiness, he regretfully returned to the beach, where he partook of a hearty meal and redonned his waistcoats". In the paintings made on this trip of the entrance to Shoreham harbour details are all but ignored. Tone and harmony predominate until, as Clothier put it: "the natural world is like a transparency" (CC 1985 30). This, for him, is the height of what he classified as a middle period in Steer's watercolours.

Further developments were called to a halt for a short while, for in the following year, 1927, illness prevailed and he underwent a prostate operation, passing the summer convalescing in Brighton. From around this time problems with his eyesight began to occur also, which meant that vision from the centre of one eye was obscured and objects could only be made out from one side. Personal problems continued for Steer at this time. In July 1929 his nurse Mrs Raynes, then aged ninety-one, finally died. She had been ill for some time and Steer had looked after her with enormous care, often curtailing his painting expeditions because he was unhappy to leave her for too long. Close friends were well aware of his concern, and of the old woman's great importance to him. Jacques Emile Blanche knew of the significance of Steer's housekeeper although he hardly knew Steer himself — all the bachelors coveted her, he wrote, "she looked after him as if he were a child and saved him from all material worries" (JEB 1937 134). According to Sickert that life was "an ideal state of affairs", modelled on the traditional customs of the old English middle classes. With Mrs Raynes as his support, Steer could conduct his ritualistic daily habits in considerable comfort. When he did go away Tonks in particular visited the house and kept him informed of her progress. Steer sent a telegram to Tonks on the day of her death, and he spoke of his sadness at the loss of a "staunch supporter and devoted friend". In 1922 he had painted her portrait, and portrait painting was a rare activity for him at that stage. With some reluctance and after much persuasion he sold the picture to the Chantrey Fund. She is a forcible presence, a solid monumental form with shrewd piercing eyes. It is impossible to overestimate the continued strength and reliability that she had provided for Steer — she was ever present from his childhood through his mother's illness, his father's death, and the years when in spite of the support of a few close friends he had suffered sharp attacks from the critics, was isolated and was frequently pessimistic. The nurse had provided Steer's security throughout most of his life. He seems to have had little contact with his own family, in later years especially. Ronald Gray commented that they were so outside his daily life that none of his friends knew them. Mrs Raynes' death marked the beginning of the real decline in Steer's own health, and the gradual decrease in his painting activities too.

From the late twenties however public display and recognition for his work reached a peak. In letters from this time he speaks of numerous requests from potential purchasers to visit his studio. But for someone renowned for a degree of 'parsimony', as Gray put it, he seems never to have been especially anxious to sell his pictures, just as he was frequently reluctant to take on commissions, and typically put people off with excuses or vague promises. Alternatively if he was unsatisfied with work he would sell for less than the agreed price at his own insistence — his supposed miserliness never seemed to apply to his own work. Similarly he was never particularly concerned to be represented in foreign collections. At one point in 1926 MacColl had succeeded in interesting the collector Joseph Duveen in buying up English artists to take to America. Duveen was already favourably impressed by Steer's work — which he included in his book *Thirty Years of British Art*, published in 1930 — and was keen to meet him at his studio. Steer seems to have been fairly indifferent to the suggestion and the meeting never took place.

From 1927 he exhibited consistently at Barbizon House, the gallery established by his earliest dealer David Croal Thompson, and run subsequently by his son Lockett Thompson. His exhibitions there in the thirties were doubtless based to an extent on the sense of loyalty which he always showed either to people or to institutions with whom he had long associations, a tendency that in some instances had not always worked to his own advantage. One striking departure from his usual exhibiting practice, however, came in 1929 when a special exhibition of Steer's work was held at the Tate Gallery, the first retrospective of painting by a living artist ever held there. Steer made the choice of work shown himself, and included the portrait of Mrs Raynes. Since MacColl's departure in 1911 the Tate had been run by Charles Aitken, who resigned the year after Steer's exhibition. Aitken had been loosely associated with the NEAC for many years, and his name always appeared on lists of those present at honorary dinners for its senior members — including Steer's, for whose work he had a particular admiration.

Aitken's exhibition policies are made clear by two descriptions of him; one from MacColl, who termed him "my memorable successor" (DSM 1945 51), and one from John Rothenstein, who viewed him as "pedestrian and unimpressive" (JR 1962 37).

In 1930 Steer finally decided to retire from his teaching at the Slade after twenty-seven years. This decision was fuelled by Tonks's resignation as Professor. Steer had remained on the staff for many years primarily to provide support for his friend who continued to rely on his judgement. It was later pointed out by Gray that since his appointment in 1917 Tonks himself had "never appointed anyone worth a damn" as an assistant. This may or may not have been dubious decision-making on his part, but it might account further for his reliance on Steer, in spite of his reluctance to impose on him and to take time away from his painting. Having had an established market for his pictures for several years, it is clear that salary was no real incentive to Steer to remain in teaching, although, as MacColl suggested, it became his habit to watch the growing snowball of his fortune. In his letter of resignation Steer stated that he had seen his services more in the "light of pleasure than work". But with the decline in his health and the absence of his close companion Tonks, it was time to withdraw. The gradual weakening of his eyesight in these years made it all the more important to him to save what there was for his own work — "the only thing of real importance to me".

Students recalling Steer's last years at the Slade invariably described a kindly old character, renowned for his quiet smile and profound still look. He was remembered as keen to converse, not simply to instruct and criticise as Tonks was wont to do. He was interested to discuss new places to paint and the varying qualities of light and colour in different areas. His actual teaching grew increasingly monosyllabic as he dragged his stool from student to student, and his advice was always given practically, taking the brush into his own hand. This approach was clearly valued by most of his class — one woman later recalled how they would rush to close windows on his arrival in case a draught on his neck meant he wouldn't stay long at their easels. Ray Howard Jones expressed the sentimental view of Steer that all at the Slade seemed to share when he commented on him in 1943:

His simplicity was greatness, his estrangement from social affairs a
natural and unremarkable thing, necessary if one lives to paint,
though not always so interpreted (RHJ 1943 68–71).

In 1931 Steer was awarded the Order of Merit, having previ-
ously declined the offer when it was made by Ramsay Macdonald in
1927. The second time he gave in to the encouragement of his
friends and accepted, although he was on the whole typically rather
uncomfortable and embarrassed by the business, finding it odd to
be honoured for doing indifferently the only thing he liked —
playing about with paints — "a job to be done in between meals".
But this was firm and final official recognition for Steer and his
friends at least were delighted and seemed to view the honour as a
personal vindication. MacColl for example congratulated him on
his O.M., pointing out that he had "had the D.S.M. a generation
ago" (DSM 1945 150).

Steer made his final summer painting excursions in the early
years of the thirties with trips to Whitstable and Sandwich included
in 1931 and to sites in Kent, Essex and lastly Hampshire in the
years following. In 1931 he painted with Behrend and Philip
Connard on the Kent coast, and this marks what has been described
as his last period in watercolours. His pictures of the sea, the
mudflats and the boats are almost monochrome, and colour drains
away into the broad thin washes of paint, as the title of one suggests:
A Calm of Quiet Colour, Totland Bay. And in paintings of Greenhithe
and Malden in subsequent years he consistently produced pictures
of such exquisite atmospheric effect that the works of his final years
can be judged finally as part of his most successful achievements.
But his eyesight worsened and the blindness that had threatened
for several years was developing rapidly from around 1935, when
the sight in his right eye also deteriorated.

An operation was impossible and the condition was left to its
natural course. Although some vision always remained and he was
still painting seascapes at Bosham in 1938, his doctor recalled that it
was tragic to witness him making his last efforts. Yet in times of real
distress Steer's natural resilience and determination always seemed
to overcome the laziness and hypochondria that engulfed him at
other times, and he was even willing to joke — it didn't matter if he
couldn't paint — "he had painted enough and many people painted
far too many pictures".

In his final years he was increasingly restricted to his house, ever more dependent on Florence Hood — the young housemaid who had been trained by Mrs Raynes to be her replacement from the age of eighteen, and who spent thirty-four years in Steer's employ — and one other maid, Cicely Williams. Those members of his old circle that remained visited religiously, Ronald Gray especially, although this last appears to have spent much of his time staying with various friends or relatives in different parts of the country; a restless, rather dissatisfied character whose letters are full of complaints and no small measure of hypochondria too. But gradually the circle dwindled. Tonks died in 1937, Brown in 1940, and MacColl's own ill-health meant that his visits were infrequent.

Much of Steer's time latterly was spent with his secretary, Miss Huggins, arranging his affairs, signing drawings and watercolours, sorting out trunkfuls of belongings which included so many memories of his childhood — toys, pieces of his mother's needlework, his grandmother's wedding dress — a rather melancholy collection and a sign of the obsessive nostalgia that dominated his life. As he got older he had begun to hoard canvas and paper, apparently buying odd shaped canvases from the Chelsea Art Store very cheaply, which to Gray accounted for the smallness and unusual shape of many of his later pictures. Otherwise his time was taken up with local shopping trips accompanied by his dog and cat, answering letters — a loathsome occupation for him — and visitors. Amongst the latter apparently were a series of young women — some ex-students or models, some family connections — all of whom regarded him with great affection. With a flash of his occasional paranoia, Steer felt they were visiting with an eye to a wedding present, hopefully a picture, and he is supposed to have stamped on this possibility by sending one such hopeful a handful of carefully chosen shells from his collection.

His potential for endurance reached a peak towards the end of his life, when he elected to stay on in Chelsea throughout the Blitz, to be "with my things" as he put it. Bombing raids along the river made his position in Cheyne Walk especially vulnerable, and several of his favourite buildings in the area were razed to the ground. His nights were spent in his basement, transformed into a draught-free anti-gas chamber where he sat fully clothed all night for almost two years waiting for a bomb to hit the house. It was never in fact hit, but vibration from nearby blasts blew in windows and damaged the roof badly. One visitor from these years expressed the irony, as she saw it, of Steer at the end of his life, enduring long nights like these in the basement instead of taking his chances and sleeping at least in some comfort in his own bed.

Recollection and Reassessment

Steer died on 18 March 1942, having failed to recover from a prolonged attack of bronchitis. He was 82. His request for cremation was carried out at a very small service at Golders Green. He had stipulated no tombstone, but a memorial tablet was placed in Painters Corner in St Pauls. A 'Steer' medal to be awarded at the Slade School was also planned, and the design and execution of this caused considerable argument amongst those involved, reflected in Gray's letters to MacColl. Gray was named along with Sir Alec Martin as trustee and executor to Steer's estate. The large extent of this surprised all, in spite of his famous carefulness in financial matters. Money and property were divided among friends and relatives, with small legacies to two charities. Letters and other papers were left to the discretion of his niece Dorothea Hamilton.

Several of his paintings, and his collection, were bequeathed to particular individuals and some to institutions. A bronze bust of Steer by Stirling Lee he wished to leave to the Tate, but this was turned down by the then Director, John Rothenstein. His decision led to an outburst of anger and extremely racist comment, from Gray in particular. Gray and Martin were to deal with the large quantities of unfinished sketches, watercolours and drawings, with strict instructions to ensure that no work detrimental to Steer's reputation should come onto the market. Much of this collection went into the sales of the remainder of his effects held at Christie's in 1942. Gray was especially annoyed later by the decision of Christie's to display the watercolours in portfolios rather than on screens, which, as he thought, played into the hands of the dealers. Two sales were held at Christie's in July 1942, the first of pictures and the second of furniture and objects. The coin collection which he had built up throughout his life was sold in the October, and all three sales, including probate, totalled almost £114,000.

132

In July and August of 1943, Steer's memorial exhibition was arranged by the Tate but was held at the National Gallery, which had put rooms at the Tate's disposal during the war. MacColl remarked that war conditions made assembly of the exhibition difficult. The collection formed by Augustus Daniel, an early NEAC patron and friend of Steer, was absent, and in MacColl's estimation too many second-rate works were included.

The shifts in critical opinion of Steer immediately after his death and in subsequent years are interesting not simply in terms of changing assessments of the painter himself, but also in terms of the developing view of British art in general in that period, and as an indicator of the personal preoccupations of the writers concerned. Just after his death the question arose of who would write Steer's biography. In his lifetime Steer had dismissed the idea, believing that no-one knew him well enough, a not inconsiderable point. But afterwards friends like Geoffrey Blackwell and Steer's niece Dorothea Hamilton were insistent. MacColl was of course the first choice, but his declining health put the question at issue. He had become weakened ever since earlier, unfounded, suspicions of tuberculosis, and the loss of his son in the war took its toll. After a bout of illness he relinquished the task in its early stages. The sheer practical problems in wartime and immediately afterwards, with paper and other shortages prevalent, were also a handicap. For a time Dorothea Hamilton was herself a possible choice, though not one widely approved of. And Tonks's biographer Joseph Hone actually began the work at one stage although with many reservations. MacColl's recovery and change of heart were greeted with relief by what remained of the Steer circle, and by Hone also.

The basis of MacColl's book was the short biography for the 'Artwork' series, of which MacColl was the editor, which had been published in 1929. At this time Tonks and Brown had written their own memories of their early days and experiences. This earlier 'sketch' as MacColl described it was expanded via the letters and correspondence then in Dorothea Hamilton's possession, augmented with the vast amounts of reminiscences supplied by Steer's friends, ex-students, painting trip companions and so on.

G.L. Behrend, Geoffrey Blackwell and Ronald Gray provided the bulk of this material. Gray, it seems, may perhaps have undertaken the work himself, except that he appears to have been rather unsuccessful as a writer, never managing to find a publisher for his reminiscences of Chelsea in the 1890s for example. Alfred Yockney, who prepared the catalogue of Steer's paintings, was also given the task of carrying around MacColl's lengthy questionnaire to relevant individuals. Gray, at one point, suggested that Yockney and he were doing most of MacColl's work for him.

The publication of the book in 1945 however was awaited with much anticipation by interested parties, and was roundly praised on its appearance. It is an extremely interesting work, an affectionate and well-researched portrait of his friend. But, needless to say, it is also a very biased judgement of his paintings, often excessively so. MacColl's personal stance and his own period preoccupations frequently obscured his judgement. He was known to reject opposing views too readily as mere idiocy, as his relation with Fry showed. The consistency of his attempts to pinion Steer into his own categories and to claim him for a specific tradition, and his at times bloody-minded hostility towards trends in art that did not coincide with his philosophies, all constrained him, leading to an overly partial and restricted view. This was obviously exacerbated by his difficulties in achieving any kind of objectivity towards his subject. His own preferences and critical bias ultimately hindered the realisation of the aims of the book. Likewise at times these were without doubt a hindrance in several respects to Steer in his lifetime.

In the early pages of the biography MacColl himself commented that he was not naturally a historian, that he saw habitually by detached picture rather than by continuous narrative. This explains also the weakness of the book in terms of providing a more general social context for Steer, or any particular attention to painting by contemporary artists outside of Steer's clique but of relevance to the spirit of his art. By his own description he was presenting a formalist version of Steer's art but with the addition of much illuminating anecdote provided by friends in correspondence. The anecdotal information about Steer and his milieu had also begun to accumulate in the thirties, with the publication of recollections and accounts of the era by many of those associated with the period: Frank Rutter, Alfred Thornton, William Rothenstein and A.S. Hartrick, to name a few. Two years before MacColl's book, another work on Steer had been published by

Robin Ironside under the aegis of John Rothenstein. This was essentially a volume of reproductions, and Ironside's text MacColl described in his introduction as a "useful, if not a final anthology". In private he appears to have been much less polite. 'Ironsides', as he was known, seems to have been little liked by the Steer circle, and there appears from Gray's letters to have been some criticism of the book, especially by MacColl.

Yet a reading of Ironside's text reveals little to particularly annoy Steer's circle. His comments and assessment are fairly standard. Steer is viewed as a natural, instinctive painter of the same tendencies as Constable. His art is anti-intellectual and innocent: "slumber was often the response to the conversation of George Moore, Tonks and D.S. MacColl" (RI 1943 2). Perhaps this sentence was a slight irritant. It does seem that for the most part the group of friends would inevitably be scornful of anyone outside their number attempting to write about Steer, of whom they became increasingly possessive over the years. Furthermore, this writer was too closely associated with Rothenstein in their eyes. Ironside's final perceptions of Steer's essential nature offer an interesting view of him in the context of the 1940s, when Neo-Romanticism — the movement with which Ironside was most associated critically — was the most dominant in British painting.

> His art subsists evergreen in our midst, at a time when painting is seeking increasingly a new romance in the region of personality, because it is a powerful, unobjectionable expression, without complexity, safe in the lack of any personal, philosophic or literary motives (ibid 4).

For Ironside, Steer was content to accept the loveliness of nature without enquiring into its deeper influences on the human spirit. Perhaps the question should then have been asked of Steer: how and why those deeper influences related and led to specific types of representations of nature.

Rothenstein's views of Steer appeared in the forties and early fifties in a couple of articles on him individually and in several surveys of British painting and of the Tate collection. In 1944 he described his impression of Steer made on earlier visits, his delight at the way Steer would shuffle up to a picture and give it a "shrewd forthright look as though he was a good farmer appraising a pig"

(JR 1944 202). In his chapter on the artist in *Modern English Painters* he again emphasised his "unpretentious, workmanlike approach". As with Ironside, Rothenstein seemed to share a post war affection for the apparently unselfconscious, innocent qualities of the art from another era. In his section on Steer in his survey of the Tate collection in 1962, Rothenstein noted that until the early fifties Steer was mostly recognised for his Turner/Constable influenced works; but that by the end of that decade his earlier phase, represented in the Tate by *Girls Running, Walberswick Pier*, was being rediscovered, a "phase which his most ardent advocates discounted when they did not ignore it" (JR 1962 118) — meaning MacColl especially. By the late forties and early fifties, writers like Rothenstein shared the critical view that Roger Fry had expressed decades earlier; namely, that Steer's most successful periods were those early figure subjects, the epic landscapes of around 1905, and the liquid, lyrical visions of his old age. Other work, particularly the classical genre pictures and the reworking of the eighteenth century manner were either insubstantial and weak, or mere exercises in pastiche.

By far the most severe criticism of Steer in the latter respect came from Douglas Cooper, specifically in an article in 1944 entitled 'The Problem of Wilson Steer' (DC 1944 66–71), and in the general tone of his catalogue introduction to the Courtauld Collection published in 1954. In the first instance — the article of 1944 — Cooper essentially wrote Steer off as an eclectic, who lacked artistic consequence because he had nothing to say, nothing to communicate of his own. For modernist critics like Cooper, Steer's compositions such as *The Rape of the Sabines* and *The Toilet of Venus*, these "souvenirs of Rococo and Baroque", were quite simply ludicrous, even hysterical, and utterly affected. In Cooper's view Steer had no individual formal language and was therefore continually thrown back onto that of other painters. Catastrophes, like the two paintings just mentioned, were the inevitable result. Rothenstein similarly found works like *The Pillow Fight* to be "inane and vaguely allusive" (JR 1952 67). In both instances these writers were expressing basic modernist prejudices: that painting was an evolving process, a progression of styles superseding one another without a backward glance, and were concerned purely with innovation. This is also a formalist view in itself. Picture develops after picture with no real value attached to personal or social motivations in the emergence of works of art.

Cooper's antagonism to Steer's eclecticism extended to a modernist's attack on those very qualities of Englishness that had endeared him to so many earlier critics. The constant references to Steer's instinctive abilities, always viewed previously as a positive attribute, were in Cooper's view quite the reverse. For what he believed to be a general lack of artistic merit in this country, both historically and at the time of writing, he blamed just that "certain kind of Englishness" that others had observed. For 'instinct' and 'intuition' Cooper read 'amateurism'. And in this context he included Richard Wilson, Constable, Turner, Girtin and Cotman, all of whom were "thoroughly British" in their approach, which was "direct and unintellectual, sensuous and lyrical, curious but *bien éléve*". In his view amateurishness allowed an artist like Constable to ignore tradition and to take liberties in his paintings. For Cooper weakness would inevitably arise from this lack of formal idiom and discipline. As he put it: "delicate sensibility and natural instincts . . . were . . . incompatible with organised form and the professional approach".

As one would expect, Steer's supporters were outraged at the appearance of Cooper's article. George Behrend termed it a juvenile and arrogant attack and was furious that a supposedly respectable journal like the *Burlington Magazine* should have published such offensive rubbish. But writing from his particular position and critical prejudice, Cooper's response was predictable. A more considered approach now would judge it not only arrogant but foolish to dismiss pictures as irrelevant simply because they cannot correspond with one specific notion of artistic worth. What is so interesting about Steer's work is its unconscious reflection of contemporary cultural preoccupations, and the development of his painting by his personal standards, rather than by the external logic prescribed by others.

Herbert Read issued a response to Cooper's article about Steer in the same edition (HR 1944 129). He didn't necessarily disagree with his claims, but he was interested in why 'Englishness' should be equated with a kind of instinctive amateurism, and he found the causes to lie in the English environment, in customs, habits of upbringing and acquired characteristics which are "not transmitted in the flesh, but bred in the mind". This was a view very similar to that expressed by Walter Sickert back in 1910.

The assumptions of that brand of modernism, its account of stylistic change and its value judgements have been questioned and to a large extent steadily rejected since the early seventies. Its terms of reference have from experience appeared too restrictive and ultimately unsatisfactory. More subtle and flexible understandings have been adopted. In this context art does not need necessarily to be continually progressive to be of interest. It is also worthy of attention for the ways in which it reflects or subverts cultural meanings. Therefore Steer's *Classic Landscape* is interesting, quite apart from its technical qualities, for the way it gives shape to contemporary social experience, attitudes to cultural conditions, feelings about landscape and shared ideas about the past. Whereas for Cooper works like this are simply dispatched as an absurd hotch-potch of past styles with no forward thinking logic.

It is relevant to point out that Cooper adopts a critical, prescriptive attitude, while the opposing position relates more to a historian's perspective. However the one stance does not and need not preclude the other. The mid to late fifties stand out as a time in which particularly little recognition was given to the art of Steer's generation. The appeal of American and European avant garde painting in these years was not conducive to concern with late Victorian and Edwardian painters. Any attention given to British art was generally to abstract artists relating to the 1930s and 40s such as Moore, Nicholson, Hepworth and Nash.

In 1960 the Arts Council staged a memorial exhibition of Steer's painting. In the catalogue, written by Andrew Forge, the eclecticism and amateurism that Cooper so disparaged are seen as his most interesting characteristics. Forge stressed that he was "a divided artist", but that it was in part just that sense of dividedness: "of promise and regression, of originality and banality, of life and passivity, that constitutes Steer's fascination"; and in this he was most typical of English painting. He perceived the extent to which Steer manipulated the lessons of past artists — landscapists especially — to his own advantage, working within their example but still with personal freedom and with an intensity of vision that at times gave his subjects an "almost tragic value". In his great nostalgia for past art Forge recognised that Steer was affected by contemporary experience. His romanticism in this respect he felt allied him with the *fin de siecle* spirit — the poetic resonance of that period informed his tastes and his art. But the very possessiveness of those critics who surrounded him, who constantly sought to view modern painting in terms of British tradition, ultimately did Steer a great disservice — and he was "sacrificed mercilessly to a retrograde and chauvinistic notion of English art" (AF 1960 5–11).

Forge's particular assessment of Steer was also adopted at the time of the exhibition in an article in *Country Life* by Denys Sutton in which Steer was termed a "Gentle Artist in a Revolutionary Age" (DS 1960 1230–1). But the Arts Council centenary exhibition marked a brief interlude in a period which largely continued to ignore artists of Steer's generation. It was not until the end of that decade, and most notably in the seventies, that substantial interest in Steer and his contemporaries re-emerged. This eventually took the form of a series of monographs on artists like Sickert, Rothenstein and Bloomsbury figures. Bruce Laughton began his research at this point with a collection of articles on Steer which culminated in his book in 1971, and he has steadily maintained his interest ever since.

Laughton's book is an extremely thorough and detailed account of the development of Steer's paintings, and as such is a very valuable text for subsequent research: the present book is a case in point. But as with several other historians in the sixties and seventies — for instance Wendy Brown in her monograph on Sickert — his interests were primarily in the earlier part of Steer's career, especially in the late eighties and early nineties when he was most influenced by more recent developments in French art. In one sense then Laughton's book was a highly persuasive attempt to stake some claim for Steer in the Modernist canon. The period around 1910, though clearly documented, is of less interest to him, and Steer's late watercolours are given relatively very little attention generally, because they are on most levels outside of this mainstream process. This inevitably creates difficulties in forming an understanding of Steer and his motivation from these years onwards.

Laughton is exceptionally proficient at scholarly detection, giving much time to accurate dating and placing of individual works. This attention is aimed wholeheartedly at the examination and sourcing of the paintings themselves — which is of course praiseworthy — yet, as a result, a feel for the wider social circumstances in which Steer's personal character and experience were formed emerges with some difficulty and never entirely satisfactorily. The cultural and social preoccupations that ultimately led Steer and many other painters towards specific reappropriations of earlier British themes and traditions in landscape are not really attended to. Laughton's book, while highly admirable in many ways, is rather confining in others.

It is only when prejudice and value judgements to do with preconceived notions of artistic progress are set aside; when deviation from certain standards is no longer viewed as weakness, but as symptoms of belonging to time and place; and when the implications of the artist's own history and character are given equal importance, that fuller interpretations can begin to emerge. The problematic history of writings on Steer is a perfect example. This is not, of course, to say that focused critical evaluation is out of place — it is vital — but, from MacColl to Laughton, the writers' personal preoccupations, shaped by their own background and circumstances, have tended to predominate. Steer's massive silences, coupled with the vast range of his artistic interests, laid him open to such processes in his lifetime, and these seem to have continued ever since. The image of the painter himself, his extraordinary technical facility, the resonance of his subject matter from whichever period, and the acute interplay between his own personality and wider public experience, is lost in so many of these accounts. They can only emerge properly in an approach to history that is both objective and flexible — one that can do justice to the complex network of factors that influence an artist's output and public reaction to it. It seems to have been very tempting for writers to produce highly partial readings of Steer's work which claim to encompass the significance of his entire ouvre. This may be seen as an ironic testament to the complexity of Steer and the extent and diversity of his achievements.

Bibliography

Books

Blanche, Jacques Emile. *Portraits of a Lifetime*. J.M.Dent 1937 (JEB).

Bowen, Stella. *Laughing Torso*. London 1924 (SB).

Buckley, J.H. *William Ernest Henley: A Study in the Counter Decadence of the Nineties*. Princeton 1945 (JHB).

Bullen, J.B. (ed). *Post-Impressionists in England: The Critical Reception*. Routledge 1988 (JBB).

Campos, Christophe. *The View of France from Arnold to Bloomsbury*. Oxford 1965.

Dewhurst, Wynford. *Impressionist Painting*. 1904 (WD).

Emmons, Robert. *Life and Opinions of W.R. Sickert*. 1941 (RE).

Farr, Dennis. *English Art 1870–1940*. Oxford 1978 (DF).

Flint, Kate (ed). *Impressionists in England: The Critical Reception*. Routledge and Kegan Paul 1984 (KF).

Forge, Andrew. *Philip Wilson Steer*, ACGB. 1960 (AF).

Harries, Meirion & Susie. *War Artists*. Michael Joseph 1983 (H&SH).

Harrison, Charles. *English Art and Modernism, 1900–1939*. Allen Lane 1987.

Hartrick, A.S. *A Painter's Pilgrimage Through Fifty Years*. Cambs (ASH).

Holmes, Charles. *Constable and his Influence on Landscape Painting*. London 1902 (CH).

Hone, Joseph. *The Life of Henry Tonks*. Victor Gollancz 1939 (JH).

Jackson Holbrook. *The 1890s: A Review of Art and Ideas at the Close of the Nineteenth Century*. (HJ).

Laidlay, W.J. *Origins and First Two Years of the New English Art Club*. John Lane 1907 (WJL).

Lambert, R.S. (ed). *Art in England*. Penguin 1933 (RSL).
— *Landscape in Britain, 1850–1950*. ACGB 1983 (IJ).
Laughton, Bruce. *Philip Wilson Steer*. Clarendon Press 1971 (BL).
Lavery, John. *The Life of a Painter*. London 1940 (JL).
MacColl, D.S. *What is Art and Other Papers*. Pelican 1940 (DSM).
MacColl, D.S. *Life, Work and Setting of Philip Wilson Steer*. Faber & Faber 1945 (DSM).
McConkey, K. *British Impressionism*. Phaidon 1989 (KM).
Moore, George. *Confessions of a Young Man*. New York 1917 (GM).
Moore, George. *Conversations in Ebury Street*. Heinemann 1930 (GM).
Moore, George. *Reminiscences of the Impressionist Painters*. Maunsel 1906 (GM).
Munro, Jane. *Philip Wilson Steer: Paintings, Watercolours and Drawings*. ACGB 1985 (JM).
Rewald, John (ed). *Lettres à Lucien*. Paris 1950.
Rothenstein, John. *The Artists of the 1890s*. Routledge & Sons 1928 (JR).
Rothenstein, John. *Modern English Painters: Sickert to Smith*. 1952 (JR).
Rothenstein, John. *The Tate Gallery*. Thames & Hudson 1962 (JR).
Rothenstein, William. *Men and Memories: Recollections of William Rothenstein, 1872–1900*. Faber & Faber 1931 (WR).
Rutter, Frank. *Art in My Time*. Rich & Cowan 1933 (FR).
Stevenson, R.A.M. *Velazquez — London 1895*. Ed. Denys Sutton. 1965 (RAMS & DS).
Sitwell, Osbert (ed). *A Free House: The Writings of W.R. Sickert*. Macmillan 1947 (OS).
Theuriet, A. *Jules Bastien-Lepage and his Art: A Memoir*. Fisher & Unwin 1892.
Thornton, A. *A Diary of an Art Student of the Nineties*. Pitman 1938 (AT).
Thornton, A. *Fifty Years of the New English Art Club*. Curwen Press 1935 (AT).
Wiener, Martin. *English Culture and the Decline of the Industrial Spirit, 1850–1980*. Pelican 1985 (MW).
Williams, Ian Fleming & Paris, Leslie. *The Discovery of Constable*. Hamilton 1984 (IFW & LP).

Signed Articles

Brown, Fred. 'Recollections.' *Art Work* 1930 (FB).
Calderon, P.H. *Art Journal* 1884 (PHC).
Carter, A.C.R. *Art Journal* 1904 (ACRC).
Clothier, C.C. 'Philip Wilson Steer: Some Watercolours from the Leeds Collection.' *Leeds Art Calendar* 97, 1985 (CC).
Cooper, Douglas. *Burlington* 84, 1944 (DC).
Fry, Roger. *Athenaeum* II, 1902 (RF).
Fry, Roger. *Nation*, 10th June, 1911 (RF).
Holmes, C.H. *Times*, 22nd April, 1909 (CII).
MacColl, D.S. *Spectator*, 5th April, 1890 (DSM).
MacColl, D.S. *Spectator*, 20th April, 1891 (DSM).
MacColl, D.S. *Spectator*, 17th March, 1894 (DSM).
MacColl, D.S. *Saturday Review*, 27th April, 1896 (DSM).
MacColl, D.S. *Saturday Review*, 26th March, 1898 (DSM).
Read, Herbert. *Burlington*, 84, 1944 (HR).
Rothenstein, W. 'Recollections.' *Artwork*, 1929 (WR).
Sickert, Walter. *Studio*, 21st March, 1894 (WRS).
Stevenson, R.A.M. *Pall Mall Gazette*, 27th February, 1894 (RAMS).
Sutton, Denys. *Country Life*, 18th June, 1960 (DS).
Tonks, Henry. 'Wanderyears.' *Artwork*, 1929 (HT).

Unsigned Articles

The Artist. 'P. Wilson Steer', O.M., N.E.A.C. 1933 (A).
Athenaeum. March 20, 1906 (Ath).
The Graphic, Vol.40, 1889 (G).
Harpers Monthly, May, 1898 (HM).
Illustrated News, 7th December, 1889 (IN).
Magazine of Art. Art in January XV, 1893 (MA).
Magazine of Art. 18th December, 1889 (MA).
Pall Mall Gazette. Extra. 'Pictures of the Year', 1886 (PMG).
Times, 18th April, 1889 (T).
Times, 2nd October, 1908 (T).
Times, 3rd April, 1962 (T).